About this Book

This guide gives you an insight into the range of stunning cycling offered by the county of Cheshire.
There are ten routes included in this guide that offer a variety of terrain across the county, as illustrated below. All the routes have navigation files that are available as a free-download.

The Carden Park Route is 53km and is fairly flat with a single notable climb.

The Audlem Route is 82km and has no notable climbs.

The Tatton Park 80 Route is 80km and fairly flat.

The Portal 100 Route is 100km and fairly flat.

Laureen's Ride is a 53km waymarked horse-riding and cycling route that includes a significant amount of low-level, off-road riding – ideal for gravel and hybrid bikes (or an easy ride on a mountain bike).

The Great Budworth Route is 63km with rolling terrain and has three moderate climbs.

The Winsford Route is 60km and includes four notable climbs.

The Mow Cop Route is 48km - the clue is in the name - with one of the toughest climbs in the county!

The Big Hills Route is 54km and includes three challenging "Black-rated" climbs

The Macc Forest Route is for gravel and MTB and although it's only 33km is does pack quite a punch!

About Cheshire

Cheshire has a population of around 1 million people and comprises of four districts, namely: Cheshire East; Cheshire West and Chester; Halton and Warrington.

The terrain of Cheshire is predominantly flat, originating from an ancient sea-bed with associated salt deposits around the towns of Winsford and Middlewich. The eastern edge of the county borders with the Peak District National Park, offering challenging climbs and fantastic scenery (as per the Big Hill Route). Also of note is the Mid-Cheshire Ridge, which runs north-to-south from Frodsham to Whitchurch and offers a series of smaller climbs, such as those included in the Winsford and Great Budworth Routes.

Disclaimer

This guide is not intended for the treatment or prevention of disease, nor as a substitute for medical treatment, nor as an alternative to medical advice. It is presented for information purposes only. Use of this guide is at the sole choice and risk of the reader. The author shall remain free of any fault, liability or responsibility for any loss or harm, whether real or perceived, resulting from the use of information in this guide.

The information provided within this guide is understood to be correct at the time of writing, the author cannot be held responsible for omissions, errors or subsequent changes.

Published by UK Cycle Routes 2019

https://ukcycleroutes.com/

All text, diagrams and photographs copyright © UK Cycle Routes

No part of this publication may be reproduced, stored or transmitted in any form or by any means including photocopying or electronic methods such as email without permission from UK Cycle Routes.

Acknowledgements

Maps contained within this publication have been created using QGIS.

Elevation profiles of selected climbs have been created from Veloviewer.com

Hill ranking formula from climbbybike.com

Although the information in the guide is new and original, I would like to acknowledge the inspiration from Simon Warren and his collection of UK Greatest Cycling Climbs books (www.100climbs.co.uk).

Cover Photos:

- Front Upper: Riding across the boardwalk section of Route 568 on The Wirral

- Front Lower: Rolling hills viewpoint from halfway up Blaze Hill

- Back Cover: Bridge over the River Bollin at Styal Mill

Contents

Introduction 4

1) To The Welsh Border - From Carden Park 7

2) Southern Cheshire - From Audlem 11

3) North East Cheshire - From Tatton Park 16

4) Western Cheshire - From Portal (Tarporley) 20

5) Laureen's Ride – From Wilmslow 26

6) Mid-Cheshire Loop - From Great Budworth 34

7) The Mid-Cheshire Ridge - From Winsford 39

8) Up Mow Cop! - From Marton 45

9) Big Hills Circuit – From Alderley Edge 52

10) Macc Forest – From Macclesfield 58

Route Summary and Download Links 63

INTRODUCTION

This guide includes ten cycling routes in the range of 30-100km that start from a variety of locations around the county of Cheshire.

There are two key principles underpinning the routes in this book, which are:
1. Classified by degree of intensity of hill-climbing (see below);
2. Following country lanes rather than main roads;

Climb and Route Intensity Metrics

Hill Grading Method

The method used to grade the climbs in this book is from www.climbbybike.com, whereby:

$$\text{CBB INDEX} = 2 \times (H \times 100/D) + H^2/D + D/1000$$

H = elevation gain (m); D = distance (m)

Therefore short and shallow hills score low; steep and long hills score high; long but no-so-steep hills (or steep but short hills) score somewhere in the middle.

Using the above index method and applying to the local hills, the climb colour-grading is:

- **Black:**   Index score greater than 30
- **Red:**   Index score greater than 15, but less than 30
- **Blue:**   Index score greater than 5, but less than 15

Here is an example of how this works in practice:

- A climb ascending 200m over 2km scores 42, therefore Black
- A climb ascending 200m over 4km scores 24, therefore Red
- A climb ascending 100m over 2km scores 17, therefore also Red
- A climb ascending 100m over 4km scores 11.5, therefore Blue

Overall Difficulty of Route

Another metric used in this book for ride intensity is the ratio of total metres of elevation gain compared to the total distance of the ride in kilometres - with guideline values as follows:

Metric	Description	Colour-code
Less than 10m/km	A fairly flat ride	Blue
Between 10m/km and 20m/km	Signifies a moderately hilly ride	Amber
Between 20m/km and 25m/km	Signifies a ride with a lot of climbing	Red
Over 25m/km	A very intense ride (typically full of Black climbs)	Black

Introduction

Way-marked Cycle Routes through Cheshire

There is a multitude of way-marked cycle routes across Cheshire that constitute a network offering a great choice for planning cycling routes. The most relevant ones that feature in this book are as follows:

- Regional Route 70, (The Cheshire Cycleway), which is a 228km circular route around Cheshire East and Cheshire West; mainly on country lanes with a wide variety of terrain;

- Regional Route 71, which is a 100km (62 miles) route that runs from Teggs Nose (Macclesfield) to Neston on the Wirral. It is a mix of country lanes and off-road trails such as canal towpaths and converted old railway lines.

- National Route 5, which runs all the way from Reading in Berkshire up to Holyhead on Anglesey with a mix of road and traffic-free sections;

- National Route 55, which runs from Ironbridge in Shropshire up to Preston in Lancashire with a mix of road and traffic-free sections;

- National Route 62, which runs for over 330km from Fleetwood in Lancashire to Selby in North Yorkshire with a mix of road and traffic-free sections;

- National Route 573 (also labelled Route 73), which runs from Congleton to Davenham, linking Route 5 to Route 55 - no off-road;

- National Route 451 (also labelled Route 74), which runs from Wrenbury to Sandbach with a mix of road and traffic-free sections.

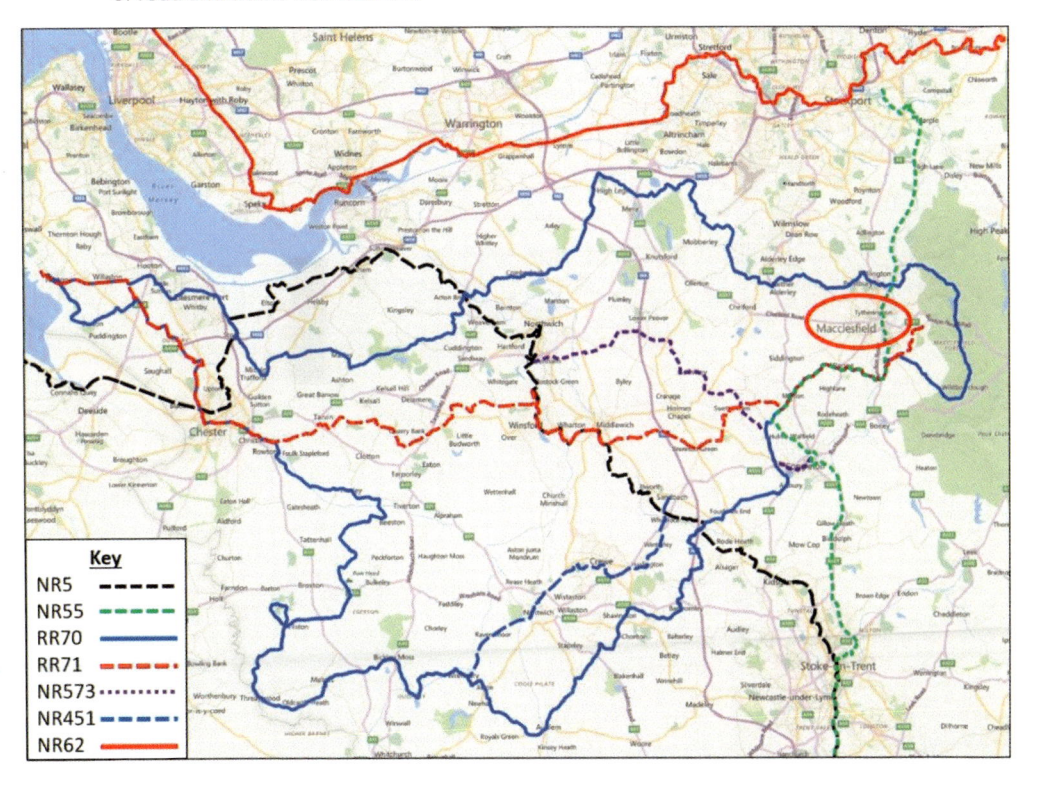

Introduction

If you like the routes in this book...

This book includes a mixture of new routes together with routes adapted from three of my other books.

Book	Description
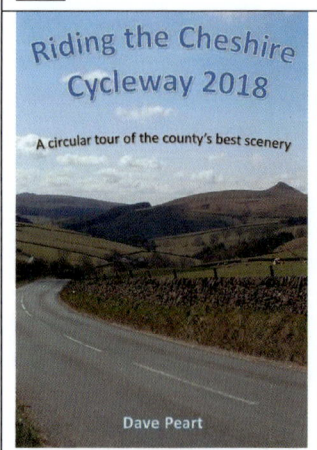 *Riding the Cheshire Cycleway 2018* — A circular tour of the county's best scenery — Dave Peart	This book divides the way-marked route into eight stages, each having start/finish points in towns or at specific cafés. The stages also have short-cut options, enabling a pick-and-mix approach to planning your ride. The shortest combination is 179km (111 miles) and the longest is 287km (179 miles). The key benefit of a circular route is being able to join at any point that is convenient! Practical information is included such as train stations, accommodation, bike shops, pubs and cafés. The routes are available to download for navigation purposes. The book also outlines five example shorter routes that incorporate sections of the waymarked route, three of which are included (with much more detail here) in this book. https://ukcycleroutes.com/cheshire-cycleway
 *Serious Cycling: Macclesfield* — Ranging from Cheshire-Plain-flat to brutally steep... 22 stunning cycling routes to challenge and delight — Dave Peart	This book comprises a collection of carefully crafted routes, graded like ski pistes from blue to black. The blue routes avoid the climbs and range from 50-200km; the red routes are hilly but avoid the really steep climbs and range from 50-100km; the black routes deliberately target the toughest climbs - the toughest route has over 3000m of elevation gain. Practical information is included such as nearby train stations, bike shops, pubs and cafés. Detailed route maps are included, and all the routes are available to download for navigation purposes. Also included are five routes for gravel bikes that mix on-road with bridleways to further your adventure. Two of the routes are included within this book. https://ukcycleroutes.com/serious-macc/
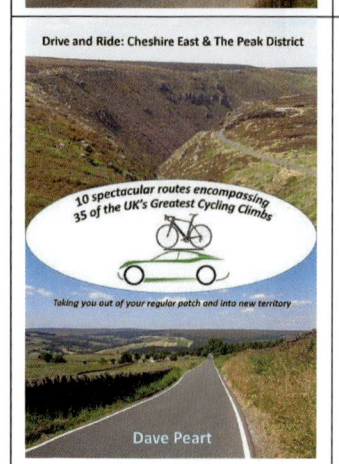 *Drive and Ride: Cheshire East & The Peak District* — 10 spectacular routes encompassing 35 of the UK's Greatest Cycling Climbs — Taking you out of your regular patch and into new territory — Dave Peart	With a wealth of scenic lanes and challenging climbs across Cheshire East and the Peak District, it makes sense to load the bike in the car, drive to the edge of your regular routes and discover a new world of cycling – one such example (Winsford) is included in this book. This book contains 10 spectacularly-scenic routes from a variety of start-points that are 30-60 minutes' drive away from the Macclesfield area. The routes are also challenging in nature - encompassing 35 of Simon Warren's UK Cycling Climbs, including icons such as Winnats Pass, Pea Royd Lane and the Riber. Each route is individually described and illustrated with colour maps, photographs and hill profiles. Details are also provided for parking and cafés around the route. Shorter versions of each route are also included as well as links for navigation files for free-download. https://ukcycleroutes.com/drive-and-ride/

1) TO THE WELSH BORDER - FROM CARDEN PARK

Dist. (km)	Elev. (m)	*m/km*	*Miles*	*Feet*
53.3	433	**8.1**	33.1	1421

Route Start-point: Carden Park Hotel

Alternative Start-points: Bickerton, Wrenbury, Marbury or Malpas

Stop-off Options: Dusty Miller (Wrenbury), Old Fire Station Café (Malpas), Carden Arms (Tilston).

This route starts and finishes at the Carden Park Hotel (ideal if you are staying over or can park your car there for the day – it is also a very picturesque location as per the photo below).

The route has a Blue intensity metric of 8.1m/km and contains only one notable climb, which just breaks into the Red category with a CBB Index of 15.3.

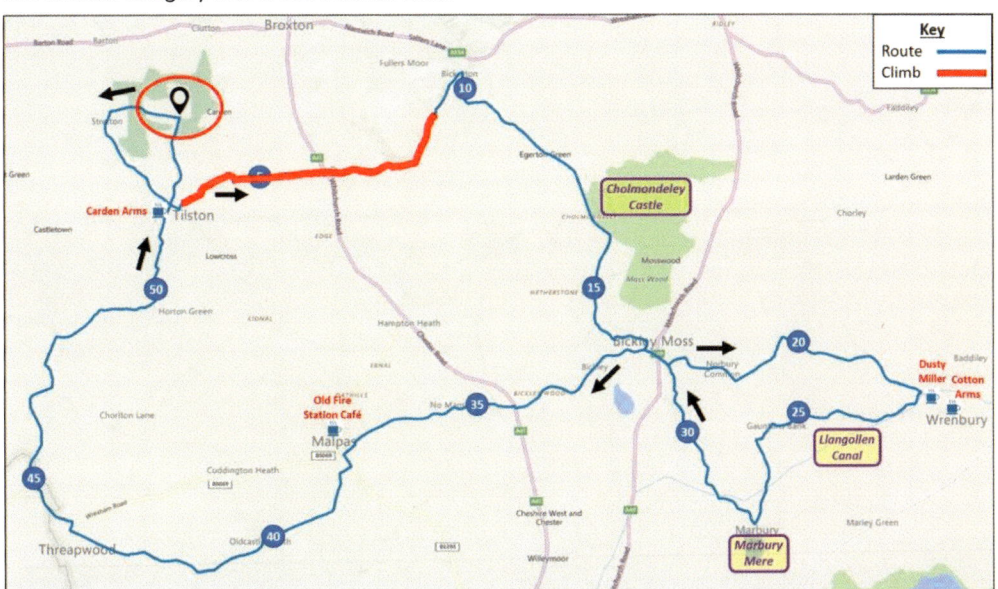

The Low-down on the Climbs

The elevation profile for the route is illustrated in the diagram below, highlighting the climbs.

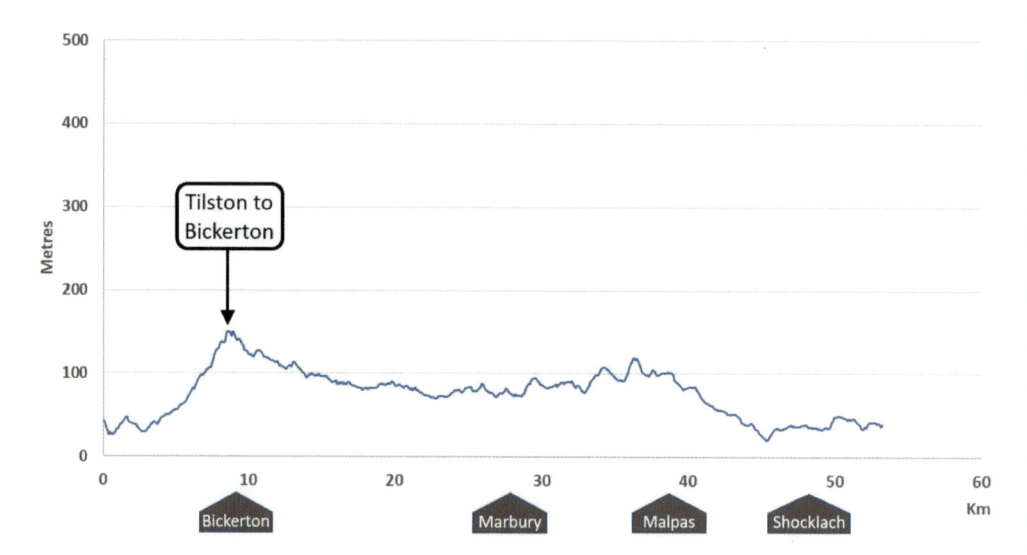

The vital statistics for the climb are summarised in the table below.

Climb	Dist. (m)	Elev. (m)	Peak Gradient	CBB Index	Notes
Tilston to Bickerton	4800	146	12%	15.3	Long and steady climb with a few steeper sections

Places of Interest on the Route

Cholmondeley Castle

Pronounced "chum-lee", this is a gothic-style castle that was built around 1800 on a site that has been the residence of the Cholmondeley family since the Norman era. The castle and garden are open for visitors with a range of family attractions, there are also large events held here through the year, including Cholmondeley Power and Speed - with racing cars, bikes and an air-show display.

Shropshire Union Canal, including the Llangollen Canal

This canal starts in Wolverhampton and provides a link between the canals of the West Midlands up to the Manchester Ship Canal at Ellesmere Port. The canal has a "main line" (from Wolverhampton through to Ellesmere Port) and additional "branch lines" such as the Llangollen Canal, which joins with the main line at Hurleston Junction - a few kilometres to the north of Nantwich.

Marbury Mere

There are five large lakes (or meres) near Marbury, the larger ones were created by glaciers during the last ice age. The meres support a wide range of wildlife and are popular attractions for walkers, birdwatchers and anglers.

Route Narrative

From the hotel, the route goes anti-clockwise around the quiet lanes of the mini-loop at Tilston and then continues along the waymarked Cheshire Cycleway (Route 70) towards Duckington and onto the only notable climb of the ride, as illustrated below.

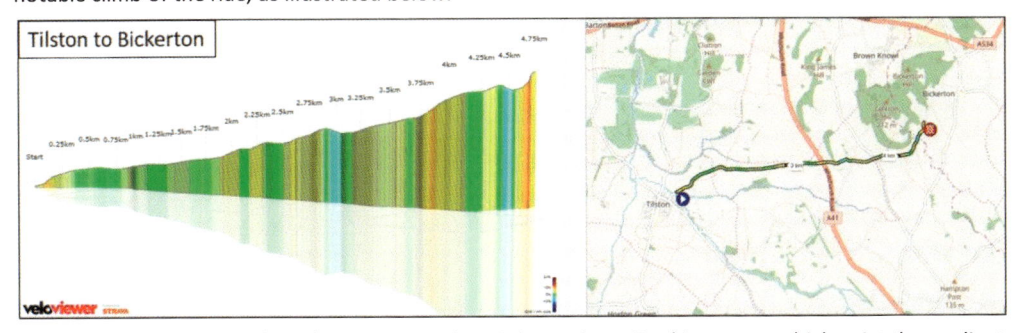

The climb starts fairly gently and crosses over the A41 just prior to Duckington, at which point the gradient ramps up slightly before easing for the junction with Coach Road. After the junction the gradient increases again and the route turns towards the north as it rounds the side of Bickerton Hill – a Site of Special Scientific Interest, which also forms the southern end of the Mid-Cheshire Ridge.

The route reaches its highest point of 152m above sea-level at the village of Bickerton and offers fantastic views over to the east (photo below).

At the following junction, the route leaves the Cheshire Cycleway and joins National Cycle Route 45 to follow Bickerton Road for the next 5km (3 miles), passing by the entrance to Cholmondeley Castle. A right turn onto Grotsworth Lane then takes you down to Bickley Moss, staying on Route 45 to cross the A49 and turning onto Common Lane through Norbury Common and on towards Wrenbury, which has a choice of places to stop for refreshments should you wish.

The Welsh Border – From Carden Park

Just before you reach the Llangollen Canal (by the lifting-bridge and the Dusty Miller pub), the route turns right, re-joins the Cheshire Cycleway and continues onto a scenic lane alongside the canal (photo below).

The route then turns south down towards Marbury, crossing over the canal and turning right just before the village to head north and back over the canal.

You then briefly retrace the outbound route as you cross over the A49 but then bear left to continue to follow the Cheshire Cycleway over a series of rolling ups-and-downs to reach Malpas – another option for refreshments.

The final part of the ride includes a gradual 8km (5 miles) descent to reach the Welsh border (photo below), before crossing back into Cheshire.

The route then passes through Shocklach, which has an ancient oak tree with a girth of 6.5m and St. Edith's church that dates from 1150. The next place to note is Tilston, whereby you dog-leg across the junction by the Carden Arms and return to the hotel for the end of the route.

2) SOUTHERN CHESHIRE - FROM AUDLEM

Dist. (km)	Elev. (m)	m/km	Miles	Feet
82.0	551	6.7	51.0	1808

Route Start-point: Audlem

Alternative Start-points: Wybunbury, Sandbach, Middlewich, Winsford, Nantwich

Stop-off Options: several cafés in each of the larger towns (Sandbach, Middlewich, Winsford, Nantwich)

This route starts in Audlem and follows the Cheshire Cycleway anticlockwise to Alsager, then joins National Cycle Route 5 to Winsford, after which it follows National Cycle Route 552 all the way to Audlem.

It has a Blue intensity metric of 6.7m/km with no notable climbs.

Note that this route contains several off-road sections that can be ridden on a road bike – but these sections may become muddy after wet weather.

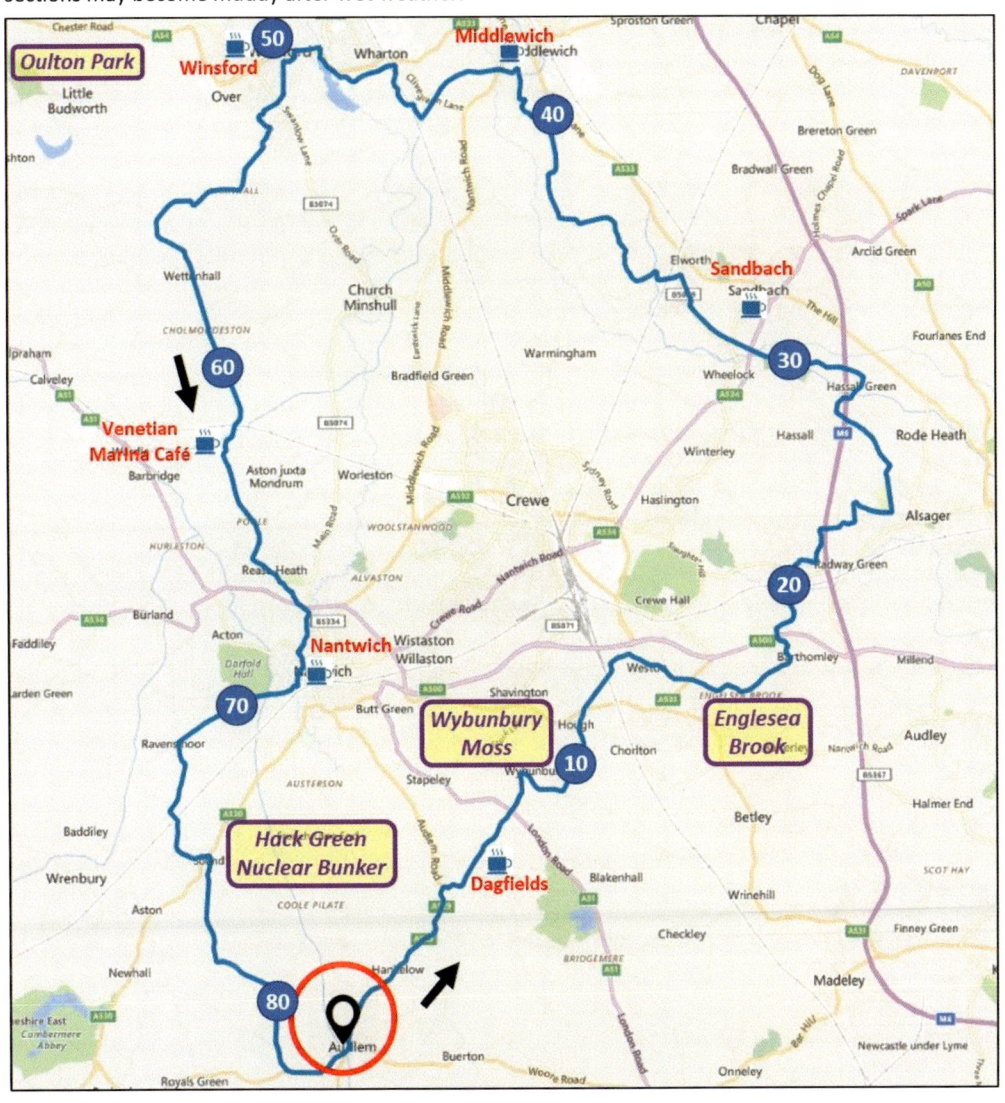

The Low-down on the Climbs

The elevation profile for the route is illustrated in the diagram below, there are no notable climbs on this route.

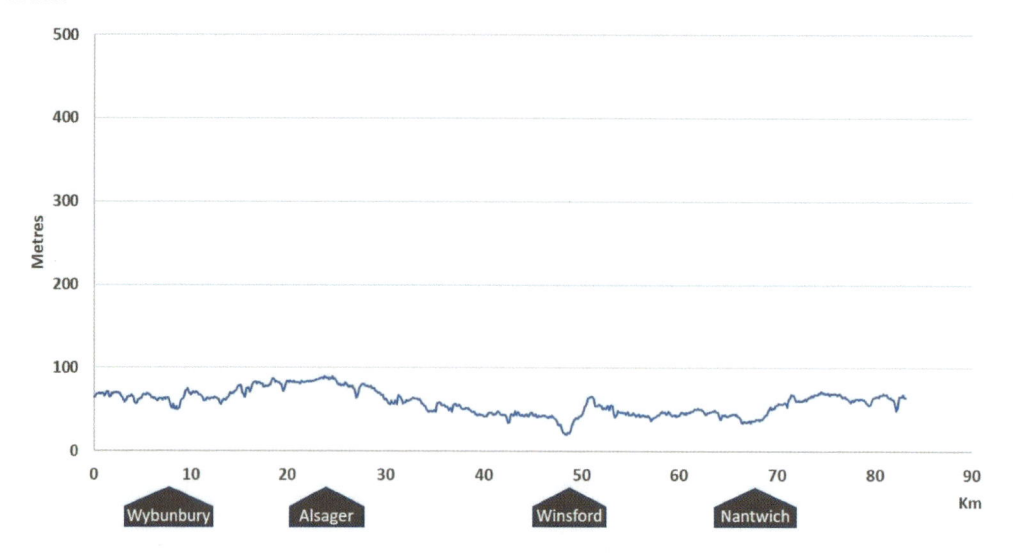

Places of Interest on the Route

Hack Green Nuclear Bunker
This was converted from a Top-Secret Regional Government Headquarters, designed to sustain existence after a nuclear war, to a museum in 1998. Its history includes a role in World War II, radar defence in the 1950s and also for military air traffic control. It was operational in its HQ function from 1984 to 1992. The museum contains a wide collection of cold war artefacts as well as a large collection of decommissioned nuclear weapons.

Wybunbury Moss
This Site of Special Scientific Interest is a lowland peat bog that was formed after the last ice-age, around 8,000 years ago. An unusual feature is that the peat structure floats on top of a 12-metre deep basin filled with water. The Moss is home to a wide variety of wildlife, including grass snakes, common lizards and many birds such as the woodcock.

Englesea Brook Chapel and Museum
The chapel is one of the earliest of the Primitive Methodist Movement, it was built in 1828 and is a Grade II listed building. There is a monument to Hugh Bourne, founder of the movement, who is buried in the churchyard. The museum is housed in the old school building, which dates from 1914; it also has a shop, café and toilets.

Oulton Park
This is Cheshire's motor racing circuit that was opened in 1953 and has hosted many Formula 1 races during its history. It is now owned by MotorSport Vision and primarily hosts British Touring Car and British Superbike Championships.

Southern Cheshire – From Audlem

Route Narrative

From the centre of the village of Audlem, the route heads north, following the Cheshire Cycleway along the A529 through Hankelow to reach Hatherton. You then turn right onto the B5071 and ride past Laurels Farm – home to Joseph Heler's Cheese, and then past Dagfields Crafts and Antiques (which has a great café should you wish to stop).

After crossing the A51, the route then leads into Wybunbury (pronounced "Wim-bree"), which is one of the oldest recorded settlements in Cheshire and was part of the Anglo-Saxon region of Mercia. Watch out for the leaning church tower (adjacent photo), which was originally built during the 15th century and whose lean was stabilised back in 1832 and then again in 1989 with a base of reinforced concrete.

The route continues along the meandering Cheshire Cycleway, passing through Hough and Weston to cross over a bridge over the A500 and on to reach a level crossing, which involves a dismount to negotiate the gate (see photo below - the barriers are normally closed but there is a signal light and a side gate to use to cross the track).

Southern Cheshire – From Audlem

On reaching the outskirts of Alsager, you encounter the first of the route's off-road sections, which crosses back over the M6 motorway and joins Alsager Road, for a third crossing of the M6.

The route now leaves the Cheshire Cycleway to join NCN Route 5, which leads to Malkins Bank and the start of the second off-road section – this time along the Wheelock Rail Trail, which runs for 2km. There is a gravel path for the first part of this section and a tarmacked path for the rest, as per the photo below.

From Ettiley Heath, the route becomes more rural as it follows a series of winding lanes in a northerly direction to reach Middlewich.

After navigating through a residential estate, there is a sharp left turn immediately prior to Shropshire Close that leads down to the towpath of the Shropshire Union Canal for more off-road riding. The route follows the towpath for almost 3km and turns off onto a gravel lane that leads onto Clive Back Lane. After a kilometre, there is a left turn onto Rilshaw Lane for 1.5km, but ensure you turn left onto a gravel track just before the lane crosses over the Winsford By-pass.

Follow the track down (it can be slippery if covered in leaves, so take care) and along to the river, then follow the cycle lane underneath the first part of the roundabout and up to cross over the river at the far end of the roundabout. The route now leaves Route 5 and joins Route 552 for the rest of the way. Continue along the cycle lane to join Winsford's High Street and proceed to the far to reach Dingle Lane and cross over the A54.

The route then passes around Winsford Cross Shopping Centre to join Dene Drive, which has a gentle uphill gradient of around 3% and continues onwards to the junction with Swanlow Lane, whereby you cross over the junction onto Townfields Drive.

Southern Cheshire – From Audlem

The route now becomes very rural as you leave Winsford behind, pass by Ashcroft Airfield to round the corner to Wettenhall and commence a 4km straight run down to cross over the Shropshire Union Canal by the Venetian Marina, which also has a great café if you choose to stop (photo below).

The route passes through Reaseheath college and emerges on Millstone Lane to cross the River Weaver before joining the wonderful tarmacked off-road cycle path (photo below) alongside the river through Nantwich – another location with a selection of cafés if you wish to stop.

You then cross back over the River Weaver, cross over an island in the river and return to the road on Queen's Drive to leave the town in a south-westerly direction.

Just after passing the Farmers Arms in Ravensmoor, the route turns right and follows Sound Lane to the hamlet of Sound, which has records dating from 1310. You then cross the A530 and continue south along Heatley Lane, which leads down to Coole Lane, and in turn onto the A525 for the final return into Audlem.

North East Cheshire - From Tatton Park

3) NORTH EAST CHESHIRE - FROM TATTON PARK

Dist. (km)	Elev. (m)	m/km	Miles	Feet
80.5	629	7.8	50.0	2064

Route Start-point: Tatton Park

Alternative Start-points: Knutsford, Macclesfield, Adlington, Alderley Edge

Stop-off Options: Pastimes Café (Goostrey), Gawsworth Shop or lots of cafés in both Macclesfield and Alderley Edge.

This is an anticlockwise loop that starts in the National Trust's Tatton Park and follows a series of quiet country lanes through Twemlow Green and Gawsworth to reach Macclesfield, after which there is a stretch of smooth-rolling A-road to Adlington. From Alderley Edge, the route follows the Cheshire Cycleway through Mobberley to return to Tatton Park.

The route has a Blue intensity metric of 7.8m/km with no notable climbs.

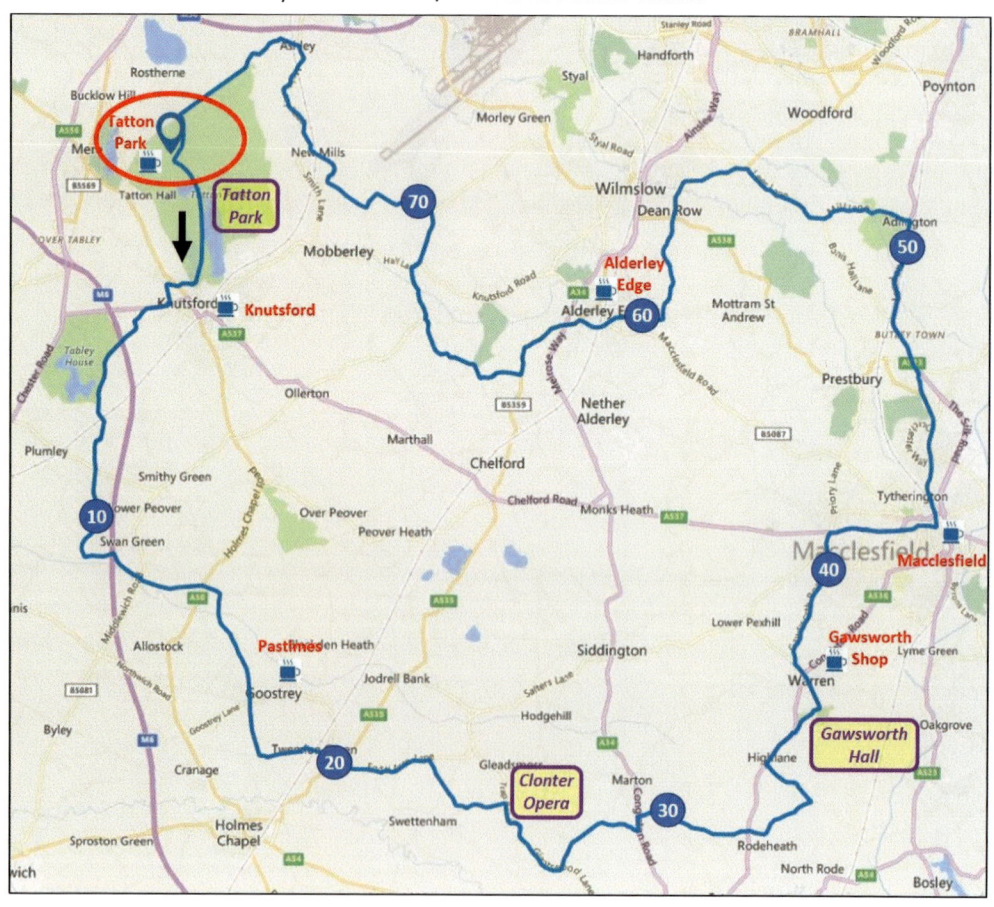

16

North East Cheshire - From Tatton Park

The Low-down on the Climbs

The elevation profile for the route is illustrated in the diagram below – there are no notable climbs on this route.

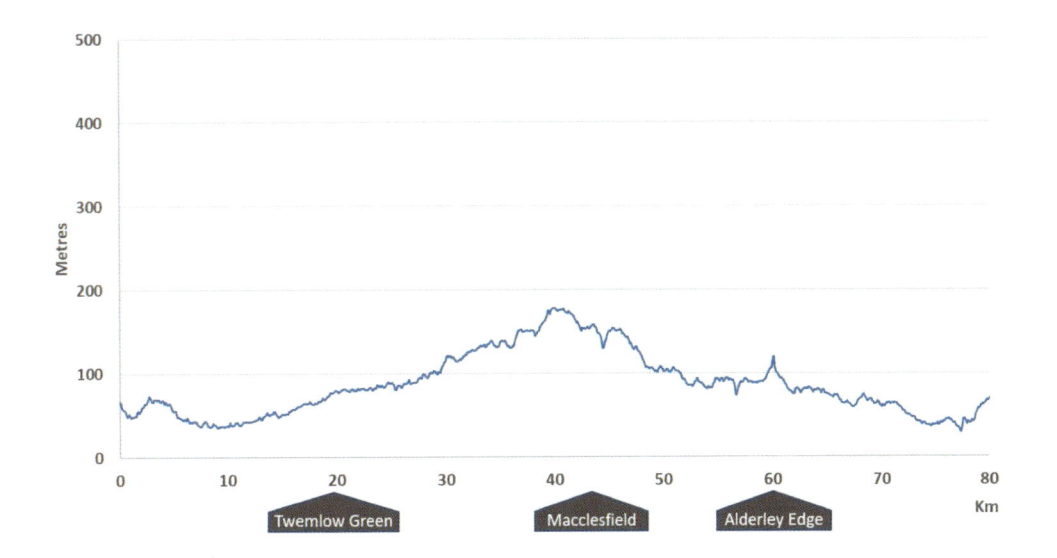

Places of Interest on the Route

Tatton Park

This was the home of the Egerton family for almost 400 years and was bequeathed to the National Trust in 1958. Its early history can be traced back to around 8,000BC with evidence of Stone Age hunting and Bronze Age farming.

It comprises a 1,000-acre deer park (photo), a neo-classical mansion, landscaped gardens, a medieval hall and a rare-breed farm. The park hosts a wide range of events every year, including concerts and was a stage finish for the 2016 Tour of Britain. There is also a gift shop, a restaurant and a café.

Clonter Opera

Located in the middle of the countryside at Clonter Farm, this a 400-seat venue that hosts 32 events each year of a musical nature; it also has a bar and restaurant. All monies raised goes to support the Clonter Farm Music Trust, which supports emerging performers with training and opportunities to perform.

Gawsworth

This is a small village in a very picturesque location, Gawsworth is home to three country houses (Gawsworth Old Hall, Gawsworth New Hall and Gawsworth Old Rectory) as well as the notable St. James' Church. Gawsworth Hall was built in 1480 and is still lived-in today. The house and gardens are open for tours, and there are fishing lakes operating a day-ticket policy.

Route Narrative

The route begins within Tatton Park (photo below) and descends to the lakes before climbing (gently) back up to the exit in Knutsford town centre. The route through the park is on smooth tarmacked roads but take care regarding slow-moving traffic and walkers.

After negotiating Knutsford town centre, the route heads over the M6 motorway and back again onto quieter lanes, circles around through the villages of Goostrey and Twemlow Green, crosses the A535 and heads deep into the countryside around Swettenham (photo below).

North East Cheshire - From Tatton Park

The way back north dodges the main roads where possible, with a brief stretch (300m) along the A34 and a kilometre along the A536 prior to a very picturesque ride through the old part of Gawsworth - past the series of pools and the 500-year old St. James' Church (photo below).

The route then crosses back over the A536 and heads towards Macclesfield along the slightly uphill Gawsworth Road, which then joins the A537 for an easy descent into the town centre. You then head along the old main road through Tytherington and join the A523 near Prestbury - this road can get busy, but during quieter times it offers swift progress as it is slightly downhill and has a good surface.

There is a left turn by Adlington train station, which leads onto quieter roads; skirting Wilmslow and heading to Alderley Edge. The route travels along the bottom of the Edge, avoids the centre of the village and heads out to Mobberley and Ashley on the Cheshire Cycleway (photo below).

There is a section after Ashley that follows the straight boundary wall of Tatton Park, it is around 1.7km long and slightly uphill (with the Strava segment name of "Tatton Wall") - the choice is yours whether you spin away at an easy pace or push hard to the park entrance at the Rostherne gate and return to the start.

4) WESTERN CHESHIRE - FROM PORTAL (TARPORLEY)

Dist. (km)	Elev. (m)	m/km	Miles	Feet
100.0	804	8.0	62.1	2638

Route Start-point: Macdonald Portal Hotel, Tarporley

Alternative Start-points: Bickerton, Beeston, Chester, Neston, Ellesmere Port, Mickle Trafford, Delamere

Stop-off Options: Cheshire Ice Cream Farm (Tattenhall), Meadow Lea Farm (Guilden Sutton), Nets Café (Little Neston), several cafés in Neston, Manley Mere

This route starts and finishes at the Macdonald Portal Hotel (ideal if you are staying over or can park your car there for the day) and follows a combination of the Cheshire Cycleway and the Chester Millennium Greenway for most of the route.

The route has a Blue intensity metric of 8.0m/km and contains five notable climbs, one of which just breaks into the Red category with a CBB Index of 15.2, as summarised in the table below.

Climb	Dist. (m)	Elev. (m)	Peak Gradient	CBB Index	Notes
Beeston Castle	1000	30	7%	7.9	Short, steady climb
Denhall Lane	800	41	8%	13.2	Short, sharp climb
Manley Lane	850	49	13%	15.2	Toughest climb of the route
Delamere Forest	3000	68	13%	9.1	Long rolling climb with two notable uphill sections
Sapling Lane	1000	48	13%	12.9	Short, sharp climb to finish the ride

Western Cheshire – from Portal (Tarporley)

The Low-down on the Climbs

The elevation profile for the route is illustrated in the diagram below, highlighting the climbs.

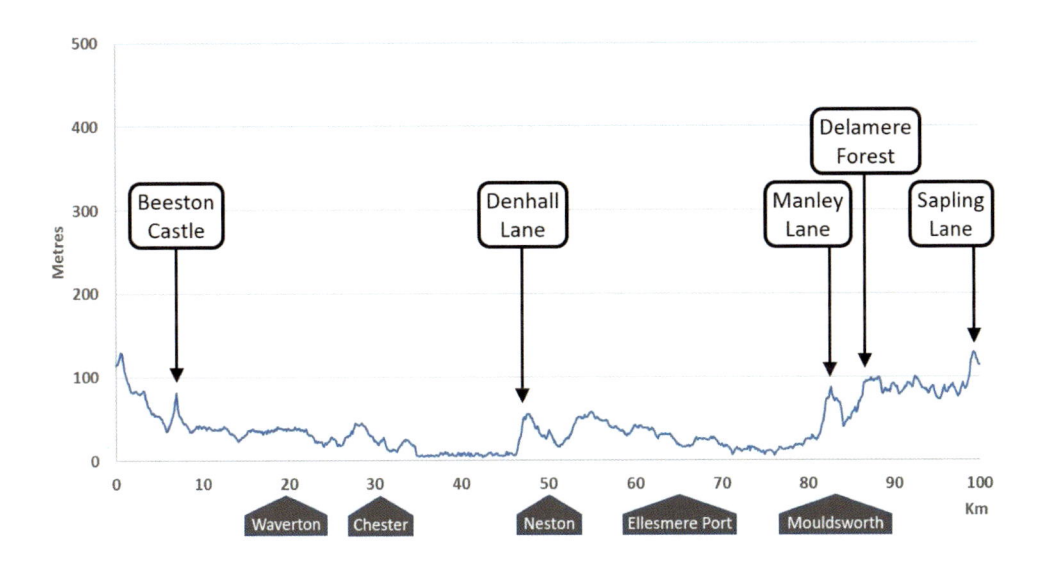

Places of Interest on the Route

Chester
The only city on the Cheshire Cycleway, Chester's history dates back to Roman times when it was established as a Roman Fort called "Deva Victrix". During this period, it was the largest settlement in England and may have been destined to become the country's capital city. It remained under Roman occupation until the Romans withdrew from Britain in 410AD.

Chester remained a significant location through the Middle Ages, in 689 Ethelred of Mercia established an early Christian church on the site that later became the first cathedral. During this period, the area took on the name of "Legeceaster", which was shortened to "Ceaster" and then later amended to its current name.

Ness Botanic Gardens
The gardens date from 1898 and were initially created by Arthur Kilpin Bulley, a wealthy cotton trader, with a purpose of cultivating plant species from foreign countries. The gardens are now owned and managed by the University of Liverpool and are open to the public along with a visitor centre, gift shop and café.

Delamere Forest
The largest area of woodland in England at 972 hectares (2,400 acres); Delamere Forest is now a fraction of its former size - it was once 160km² (60 square miles)! The use of the forest dates from Anglo-Saxon times and it has been used extensively for hunting purposes for animals including wild boar and deer.

The name "Delamere" has the meaning of a forest of meres (lakes). Blakemere, once drained in the 19th century, has been restored as a wetland environment.

There is also a visitor centre just south of the route that has cycle hire and equipment, as well as a café, picnic area and toilets.

Western Cheshire – from Portal (Tarporley)

Route Narrative

The ride departs with a short climb up the drive from the hotel to reach the road and then descends fairly swiftly through Tarporley and then continues further down to join the Cheshire Cycleway. It then crosses the Shropshire Union Canal via a narrow bridge by the Shady Oak pub and commences the first notable climb up to Beeston Castle. This is a short climb over 1km and peaks at 7% gradient, as illustrated below.

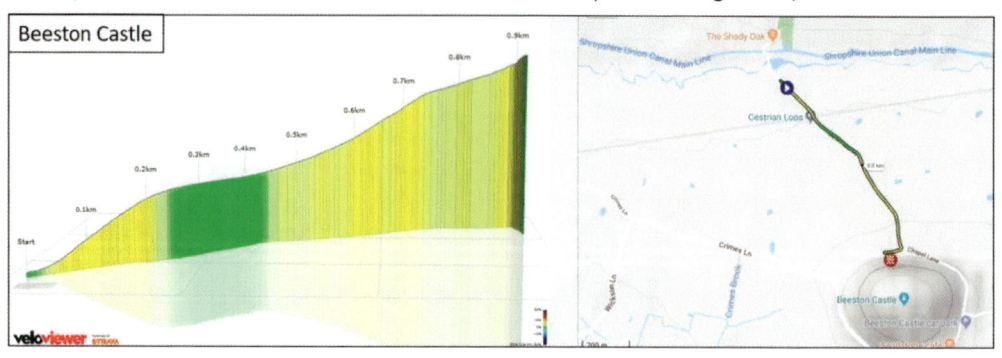

After descending the other side, the route turns right to pass the Cheshire Ice Cream Farm - worth a visit one day just to appreciate its magnitude (but not if you're in a rush)! You then cross back over the canal to re-join Route 70 on Long Lane and head to Waverton.

A series of lanes (with a busy junction to negotiate over the A51) then lead to the start of the Chester Millennium Greenway – a 14km cycle-friendly tarmacked path (photo below) with no hills and a smooth surface constructed on an old railway line with bridges & underpasses to avoid the city's roads.

Western Cheshire – from Portal (Tarporley)

To continue the traffic-free experience, the Millennium Greenway is then followed by a further 5.6km along Route 568, which includes a fabulous boardwalk section across the Dee marshes (photo below) to reach Little Neston – this is the half-way point of the route and has several options for a café stop if you choose to do so.

You then re-join Route 70 at the bottom of Denhall Lane and encounter the second notable climb, which still rates as a "Blue" but is more demanding than the first climb.

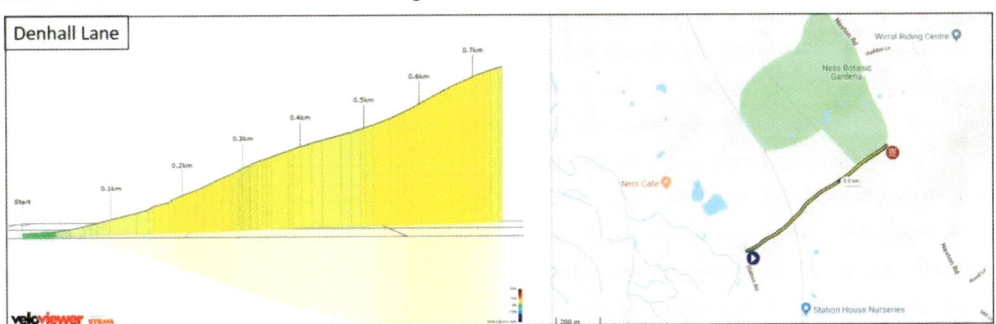

Western Cheshire – from Portal (Tarporley)

From Neston, the route follows the Wirral Way – an off-road section with a firm surface but can be prone to puddles when wet.

You then continue along Route 70 through the residential streets of Ellesmere Port but take a detour through the Cheshire Oaks Retail Park rather than joining the canal towpath of the waymarked route (you could use the canal if you wish but it is not advisable on a road bike due to its cobbled surface in several places).

After a series of country lanes and a short section on the A56, you reach Manley Mere (another good option for a café-stop if you desire) and then face the toughest climb of the ride up Manley Lane, which just breaks into Red classification.

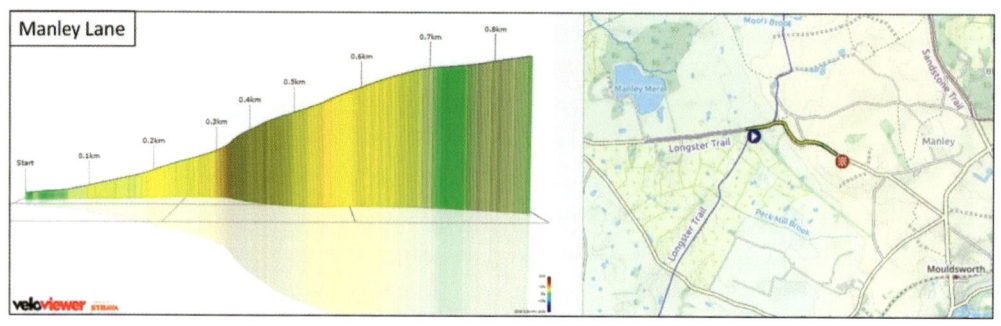

There is then a steep descent down Station Road – but control your speed in order to make the sharp left turn onto Delamere Road just before the bottom of the hill.

Western Cheshire – from Portal (Tarporley)

The next 3km are generally uphill as you approach and enter Delamere Forest (photo below) to enjoy the stunning scenery of this part of the route before reaching the junction with the B5152.

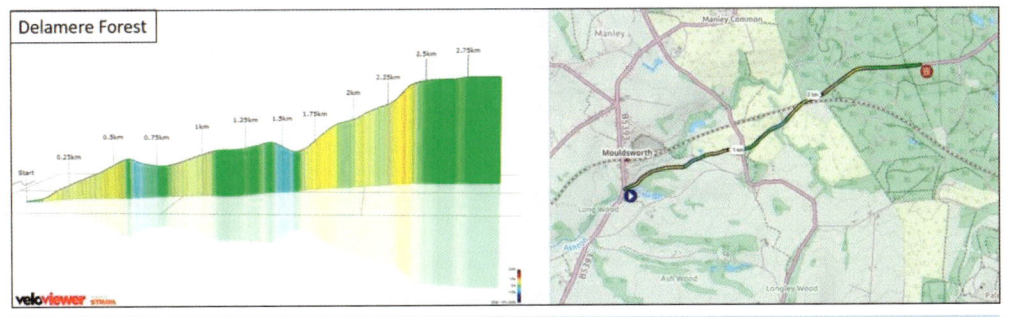

The route now heads south along the B5152, passing Delamere station and crossing both the A556 and the A54. At Cotebrook, you join the A49 briefly before turning onto Eaton Lane to reach the village of Eaton and the start of the final climb of the ride up Sapling Lane to return to the start.

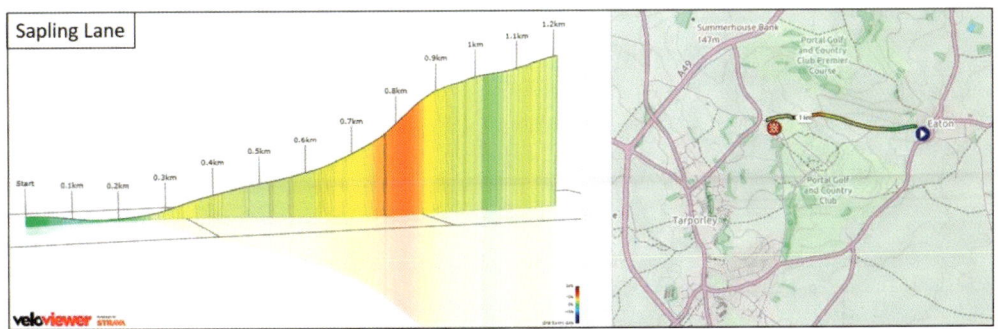

5) LAUREEN'S RIDE – FROM WILMSLOW

Dist. (km)	Elev. (m)	m/km	Miles	Feet
60.9	416	6.8	37.8	1365

Route Start-point: Wilmslow

Alternative Start-points: Warford, Mobberley, Styal

Stop-off Options: Snowdrop Café (Grasslands Garden Centre), Lambing Shed Café (Knutsford), The Roebuck (Mobberley), Church Inn (Mobberley), Cheshire Smokehouse (Morley Green), Quarry Bank Café.

Laureen's Ride is named after Laureen Roberts, a keen horse-rider from Knutsford, who designed the ride whilst off work with a broken leg in 2011 and won the support of the local council for the route to be signposted and named after her. It is primarily a long-distance horse-riding route, but also makes a great route for riding on a gravel/hybrid/mountain bike!

There are two separate routes that intersect for a short distance (see map below), this route combines both into a single ride – with a slight extension to start and finish in Wilmslow town centre.

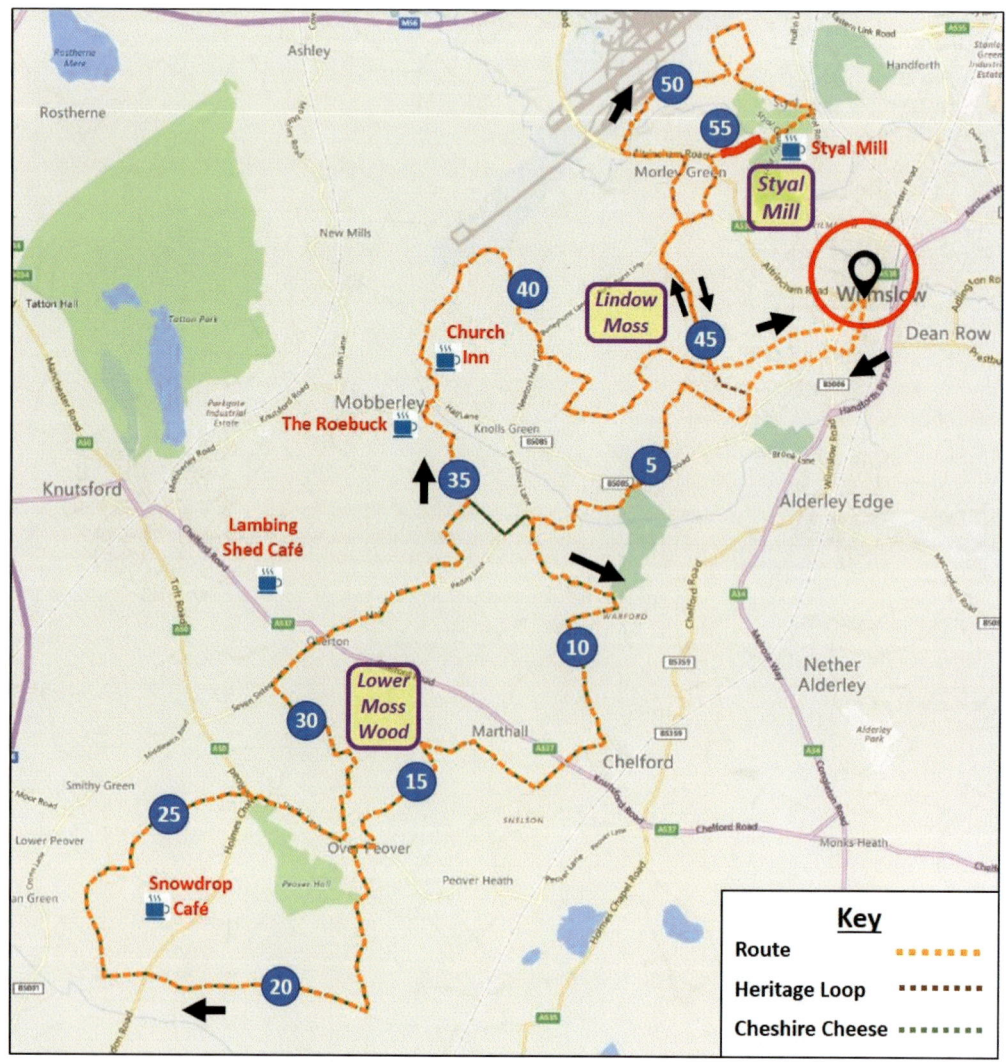

Laureen's Ride – From Wilmslow

The Low-down on the Climbs

The elevation profile for the route is illustrated in the diagram below, highlighting the climbs.

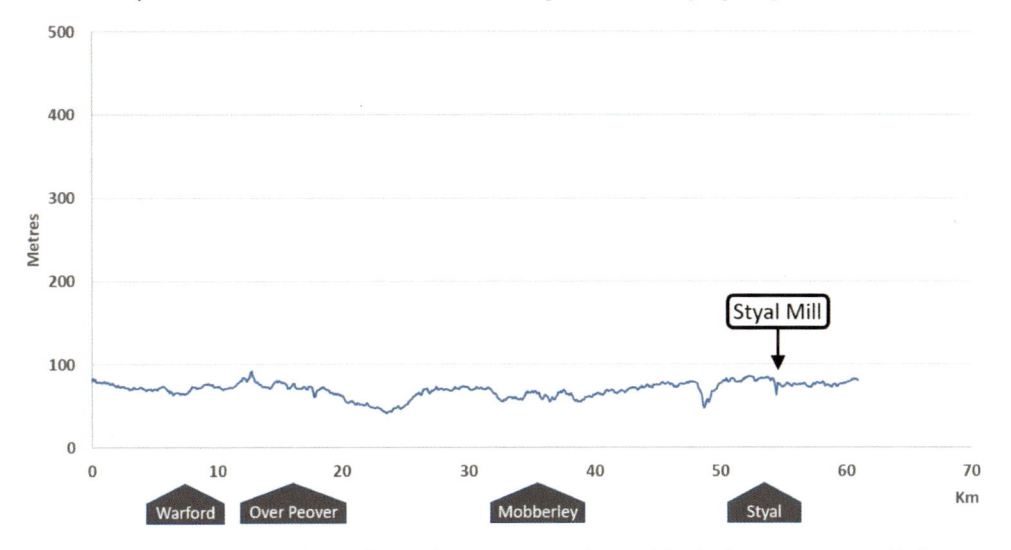

The route has a Red intensity of 6.8m/km and contains a single notable climb, as summarised below.

Climb	Dist. (m)	Elev. (m)	Peak Gradient	CBB Index	Notes
Styal Mill towards Honey Bee	200	22	19%	24.6	Short but very steep with steps

Places of Interest on the Route

Lower Moss Wood
This is an 18-acre nature reserve that also has an education facility (used by local schools and scout groups) and a wildlife hospital that treats around 2000 animal and bird casualties each year. It is also one of the most important sites for dragonflies in Cheshire.

Lindow Moss
This is a peat bog that is best known for the discovery of Lindow Man (also named "Pete Marsh") in 1984, who was brutally killed around 2,000 years ago and is the most well-preserved "bog body" discovered in the UK (complete with facial hair, manicured fingernails, healthy teeth and stomach contents). There have been several other body parts found in the peat through the process of peat extraction, including Lindow Woman in 1983 (dating from around 250AD).

Quarry Bank Mill, Styal
Built in 1784 as a factory to spin cotton, the mill is now owned by the National Trust and open to visitors throughout the year. It was initially powered exclusively by water-power from the River Bollin; a steam engine was added in 1810. In addition to the mill building, there is also an Apprentice House that tells the story of the lives of children working in the mill. The mill was also the inspiration for the 2013 TV drama "The Mill". In line with the other places of interest on this stage, there is also a gift shop and a café.

Laureen's Ride – From Wilmslow

Route Narrative

This ride starts from Costa Coffee in the centre of Wilmslow and heads south west out of the town via Holly Road South, Knutsford Road and Gravel Lane. As you approach the Horse and Jockey pub near the end of Gravel Lane, take a right turn (watch out for oncoming traffic around the bend) onto a gravel path after the pub and cut through to join Upcast Lane towards Lindow Cricket Club – you are now on the Heritage Loop of Laureen's Ride, so watch out for the purple signs!

Immediately opposite the cricket club, turn right onto a bridle path that leads out into the countryside, then turning left at the T-junction at the end onto a wider gravel track. Follow the track along around an S-bend and then bear left onto a narrow track into the trees. At the end of the path, the route joins Edge View Lane, which leads along to a junction with Knutsford Road.

The route stays on the road for the next 4.5km, which includes the intriguingly-named "Noah's Ark Lane". The route leaves Laureen's Heritage Loop at the junction with Ancoats Lane to join the Cheshire Cheese Loop on the way to that route's official start point at the start of Mill Lane (the site of the former Stag's Head pub).

Just after passing the David Lewis Centre, the route turns left onto a gated track and then turns right after 500m through a small gate into a field. Proceed across the field and down to cross a bridge over a small stream through a wooded area called "Peckmill Bottoms" – note that it can get very muddy near the stream during the wetter months. The route then joins a firm gravel track that leads up to the Dixon Drive residential estate in Chelford.

You then cross over the A537 onto Pepper Street for 500m before turning right onto the next off-road section through a wood known as "Stockin Moss", which is usually fairly firm but can become muddy in places during the winter. At the end of the path, the route turns right and then promptly left onto a narrow lane, which leads onto Sandhole Lane and then onto Moss Lane.

At the sharp right-hand bend, the waymarked route continues straight on into a field, but this is usually not navigable by bike, so this route continues along the road for a further 400m and then turns sharp left to follow a gravel track past a farm to re-join the waymarked route by the notable water tower (adjacent photo).

The route then continues along a path at the edge of a field (which can be a bit bumpy) and emerges by Colshaw Hall Country Estate and then joins Stocks Lane before turning left onto Grotto Lane.

28

Laureen's Ride – From Wilmslow

When you reach a crossroads junction, the route turns right onto Blackden Lane, which leads past the driveway to Peover Hall, continues down to cross the Peover Eye stream and up the other side to reach a right turn onto the next section of off-road bridleway.

This next section comprises 1km along a tree-lined single-track path and a further 1.4km along a farm track, both of which are slightly downhill, making for a fast and exhilarating ride – especially for the first part if you choose to pick up the pace and weave through the trees (photo below)!

The junction at the end leads onto Booth Bed Lane, which in turn takes you to a junction that crosses the A50 onto Townfield Lane and a series of further quiet country lanes that lead onto another off-road section along Sandy Lane. This time, however the gradient is upwards (but only slightly) and there are several gates to negotiate through a farmyard, plus a section of fairly bumpy cobbles. Around the half-way point of Sandy Lane, the surface becomes a bit smoother as it leads up to another junction with the A50.

This time, you join the A50 for 200m and then turn left onto Stocks Lane to pass by Barclays Bank at Radbroke Hall and Stocks Lane Nurseries before taking a left turn for more off-road riding. This section leads along a firm gravel track and emerges onto a road by Lower Moss Wood but then turns to follow a narrower path around more fields to reach a farm yard and a track that leads on to join Seven Sisters Lane towards Ollerton and the start of an on-road 2.5km section.

You cross directly over the A537 onto Marthall Lane, which drops down to cross Marthall Brook and up the other side to reach a left turn along a track that leads to an impressively-gated property (aka "Wayne's World"!). This section differs from the original route of the Cheshire Cheese Loop as the right of way has been changed and you need to bear right through a gate and follow the wire fence around to the other side of the property. The route then crosses over Pedley Brook, encounters a short sharp climb to reach Hammonds of Knutsford (an award-winning specialist drink wholesaler in a stunning location) and continues to a 90-degree bend.

This is the point of intersection of the Cheshire Cheese Loop and the Heritage Loop – the Cheshire Cheese Loop turns right to return to its start-point in Warford, however this route now turns left to join the Heritage Loop.

Laureen's Ride – From Wilmslow

The route continues alongside the edge of two fields and emerges onto a firm track that leads into the village of Mobberley via Damson Lane, which leads to Mill Lane and the picturesque adjacent Bulls Head and Roebuck pubs (the Roebuck opens for morning coffee if you fancy a stop).

The next 2.5km are along a series of lanes that cross the B5085, lead past the Church Inn and the Mobberley Brewery to join Lady Lane, which leads up to the end of the second runway at Manchester Airport. The route then turns through a gate on the right and follows a gravel track (which can be muddy when wet) for 400m to reach Ostler's Lane and onto Davenport Lane and a right turn at the junction with Burleyhurst Lane (take care at the junction regarding fast-moving traffic coming around the bend).

The next off-road section is along Graveyard Lane, which leads onto more lanes and around past the Plough and Flail pub (opportunity for a cheeky beer?). Continue along the lane and then around to the left, which leads to more off-road on a gravel path and a swift downhill section past the residential Lindow Court Park, emerging onto Moor Lane at the end.

Laureen's Ride – From Wilmslow

More off-road soon follows with a left turn onto Rotherwood Road, which leads along the edge of Lindow Moss (photo below - spare a moment to think about poor Lindow Man), past the kennels and onto Eccups Lane, with a narrow path section leading down to Mossways Park residential estate.

The road then leads up to Morley Green, crosses Mobberley Road and follows Morley Green Road to the junction with the A538 for a steep descent to the River Bollin (just before reaching the runway tunnels). It is advisable to stay on the footpath/cycle-path as you descend the hill to avoid the traffic - but take care of the kink in the path at the bottom by the bus stop. It is also advisable to dismount and cross the A538 via the islands at the bottom of the hill rather than at the waymarked sign opposite the hotel entrance.

The route then follows a path up towards the airport runway, which has a fairly steep but quite short climb that leads onto a wider gravel track next to the airport perimeter fence – offering great views of the aeroplanes.

Laureen's Ride – From Wilmslow

The track then heads away from the airport and joins Moss Lane for a mini-loop around the village of Styal, with a bit more off-road along Wilkins Lane before re-joining Altrincham Road to pass the Ship Inn and reach the junction with the B5166.

You then turn right and then right again onto Holt's Lane (the waymarked route follows the pavement for this short section) as the route heads into the National Trust property of Quarry Bank Mill (photos below). Follow the road on the approach to the mill and then either follow the waymarked signs just before the mill down a narrow, cobbled path with steps (not great unless on a MTB) or continue past the mill and cross over the next bridge over the river and loop back towards the first bridge.

Laureen's Ride – From Wilmslow

This next section contains the only notable climb on the route, which is quite challenging if you are on a capable mountain bike and near-impossible on any other bike, owing to the combination of gradient, slippery surface and a series of steps to negotiate (photo below)

It does only last for around 200m so it's not too much of an ordeal to push your bike until you reach the gate at the top.

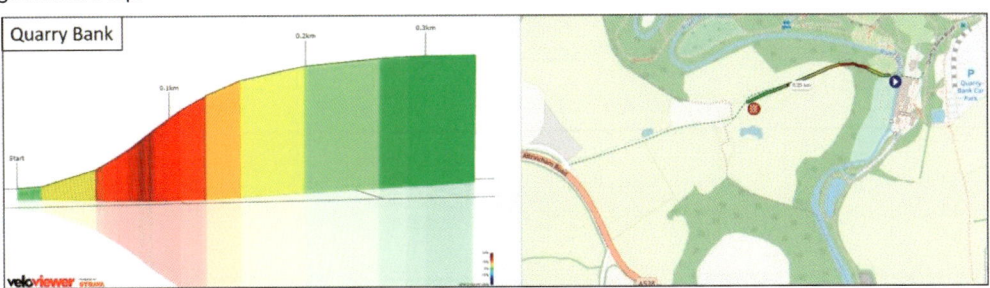

The path leads up to the busy A538, which requires crossing – head for the cycle path on the other side of the road, turn left and continue onto Nansmoss Road and then onto Mobberley Road. The following 2km retrace the outbound route back along Eccups Lane and past Lindow Moss to reach Moor Lane – here, the waymarked route heads down Cumber Lane to complete the loop, however this route follows Moor Lane, Chapel Lane and Alderley Road to return to the start-point in the centre of Wilmslow.

6) MID-CHESHIRE LOOP - FROM GREAT BUDWORTH

Dist. (km)	Elev. (m)	m/km	Miles	Feet
63.1	690	10.9	39.2	2264

Route Start-point: Great Budworth

Alternative Start-points: Acton Bridge, Kelsall, Davenham, Lostock Gralam

Stop-off Options: Davenports Tearoom (Acton Bridge), The Greedy Pig Café (Kelsall), Cotebrook Coffee Shop, Station House Café (Whitegate), Riverside Organic (Davenham), Great Budworth Ice Cream Farm.

This route starts and finishes in the very picturesque village of Great Budworth and follows the Cheshire Cycleway for the first 20km, it then heads south and takes on the climb up the Yeld before looping down through Little Budworth and joining the Whitegate Way (off-road). There is a further off-road section along the River Weaver into Davenham, where the route joins Route 573 to Lach Dennis and then heads north back to the start.

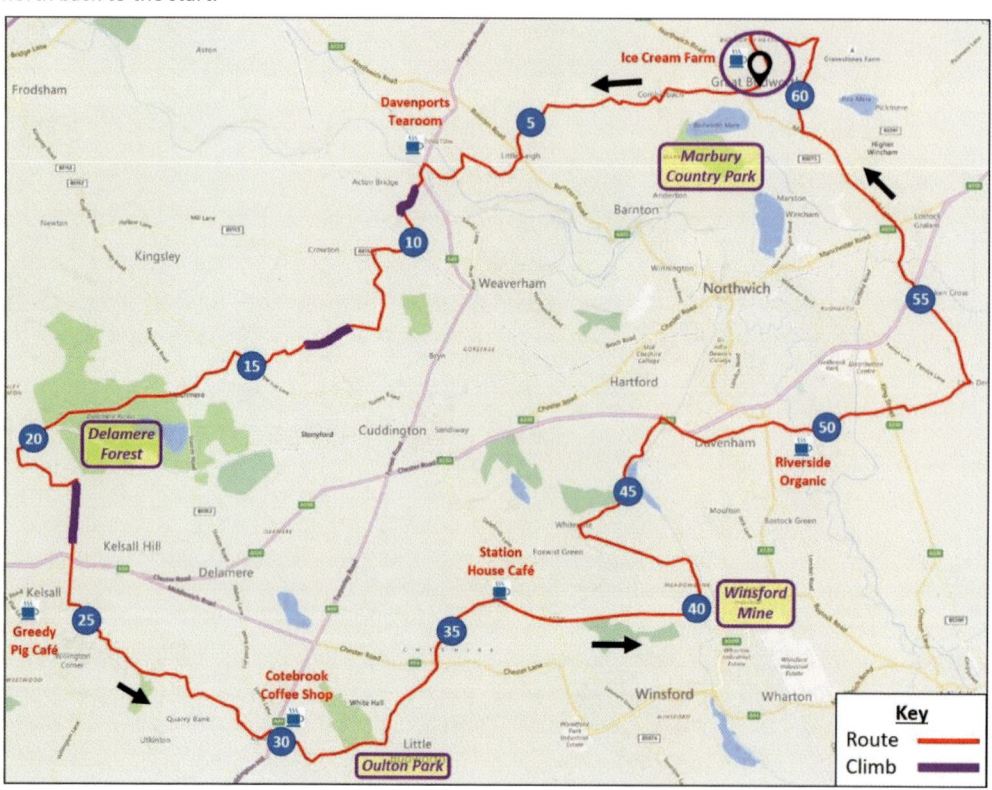

The route has an Amber intensity of 10.9m/km and contains three notable climbs, as summarised below.

Climb	Dist. (m)	Elev. (m)	Peak Gradient	CBB Index	Notes
Acton Lane	500	36	11%	17.5	Short, sharp climb
Bag Lane	800	37	8%	11.8	Steady climb
The Yeld	900	62	14%	18.9	Fairly steep along a straight road, steepest near the top

Mid-Cheshire Loop - From Great Budworth

The Low-down on the Climbs

The elevation profile for the route is illustrated in the diagram below, highlighting the climbs.

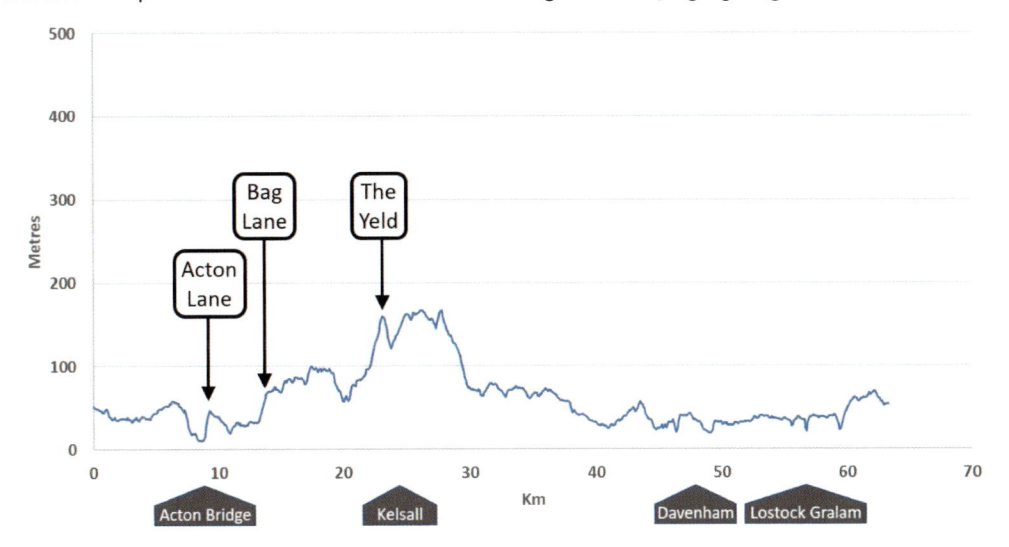

[Elevation profile chart showing climbs at Acton Lane, Bag Lane, and The Yeld; with location markers for Acton Bridge, Kelsall, Davenham, and Lostock Gralam along the route from 0 to 70 km]

Places of Interest on the Route

Delamere Forest

The largest area of woodland in England at 972 hectares (2,400 acres); Delamere Forest is now a fraction of its former size - it was once 160km² (60 square miles)! The use of the forest dates from Anglo-Saxon times and it has been used extensively for hunting purposes for animals including wild boar and deer.

Nowadays, it is a popular leisure location offering a range of trails for walkers, runners, horse-riding and off-road cycling. The forest also contains The Old Pale hill, which is the highest point of the northern section of the Mid Cheshire Ridge and is also used as a music venue. There is also a visitor centre just south of the route that has cycle hire and equipment, as well as a café, picnic area and toilets.

Winsford Salt Mine

The mine was opened in 1844, it reaches a depth of almost 200m, has over 250km of tunnels, supplies most of the salt used for UK road-gritting and has a controlled storage facility covering 1.8 million square metres!

The Whitegate Way runs along a former railway that was used to transport salt from the mine. The path has a firm gravel surface and runs for a total of 10km.

Marbury Country Park

This is an extensive country park with a network of surfaced paths suitable for walking and cycling around. There was once a hall within the park that was styled like the French chateau at Fontainebleau and was built in 1850, however it had to be demolished in the 1960s after serving as a country club, then a POW camp and a hostel for ICI.

To the north of the park is Budworth Mere; measuring over 30 hectares (80 acres), this is a popular venue for fishing and sailing.

Mid-Cheshire Loop - From Great Budworth

Route Narrative

The ride starts from Great Budworth, which claims to be the Most Picturesque Village in Cheshire (adjacent photo), largely due to the efforts of the 19th century, including the commissioning of architects to remodel several of the distinctive buildings of the village. The early history of the village dates from Norman times, St. Mary and All Saints Church (photo below) dates from the 14th century; the village has featured in several television shows and advertisements.

The route heads west down the fairly steep main street to reach the junction with the A559 (take care to brake in good time for the junction). Proceed across the junction and up the slope towards the village of Comberbach.

A series of country lanes then proceed along to cross the A533 at Little Leigh and then descend quite steeply down Willow Green Lane, passing over the Trent and Mersey Canal to reach the A49 for the swing-bridge crossing over the River Weaver.

Once over the river, the route takes a right onto Acton Lane for the first climb of the ride, which is only 0.5km in length but does peak at 11% gradient to earn a CBB Index status of Red, as illustrated below.

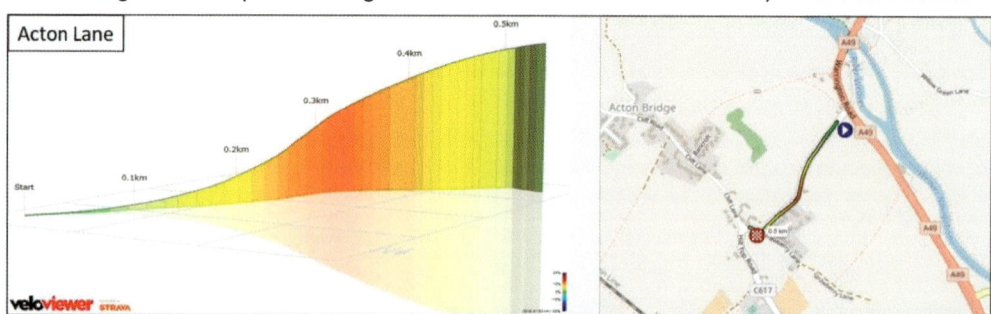

You then descend gently down with a right turn over the railway line by Acton Bridge station and then turn right onto Onston Lane, which leads along to Bag Lane for the next climb of the ride, which is longer but less steep than the previous climb.

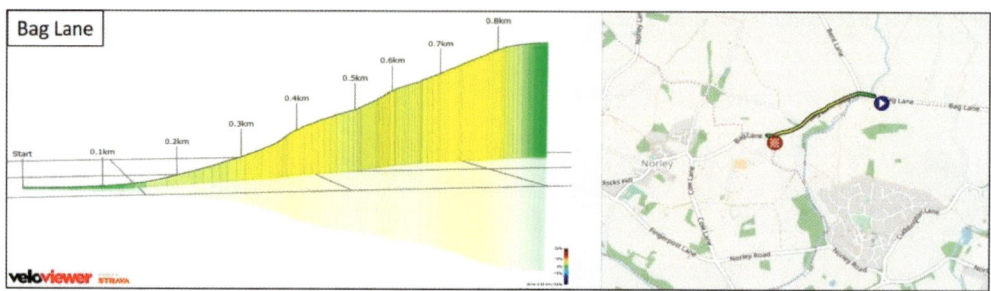

36

Mid-Cheshire Loop - From Great Budworth

You continue in a westerly direction to reach Norley and proceed on to Hatchmere to reach a junction with the B5152. The route now enters Delamere Forest and provides 3.5km of very scenic and fast-rolling cycling as you follow the rolling Ashton Road (photo below), initially slightly upwards and then quite rapidly downwards as you exit the forest and approach the junction with Brines Brow Lane.

A left turn at the junction then leads around to Farm Forest Road and then onto Yeld Lane for the toughest climb of the ride up The Yeld, with follows a very straight section of road for just under a kilometre of climbing with a pronounced kick upwards to 14% gradient for final 100m.

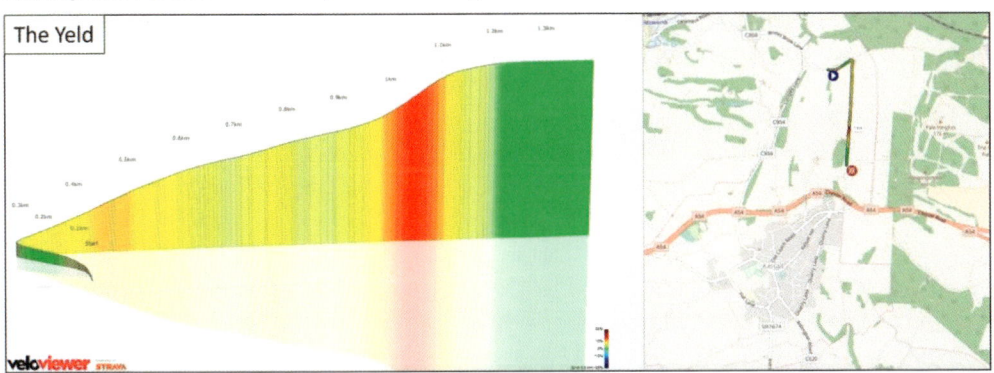

From the top of the hill, you cross a bridge over the A54 and reach a junction with Chester Road just outside of the village of Kelsall (which has a café if you wish to stop). The route continues straight across the junction onto Waste Lane, which climbs again (less steeply) up the Mid-Cheshire Ridge to reach Tirley Lane and the highest point of the route at 168m above sea-level.

Mid-Cheshire Loop - From Great Budworth

Heaths Lane leads down onto Quarry Bank, Knights Lane and Hollins Hill as you descend the eastern side of the ridge to return to the Cheshire Plain by Cotebrook (which also has a café) and then proceed past the entrance to the Oulton Park motor circuit.

The route then heads north along Park Road and Clay Lane to reach the first off-road section, which is along the old railway line of the Whitegate Way – this has a hard gravel surface (photo below), so can be ridden on road bikes, but is prone to puddles when wet.

At the end of the track, bear left and join Bradford Road, which passes next to the Winsford Salt Mine and the River Weaver before turning west and heading towards the village of Whitegate for some more off-road riding.

This next section starts with a short gravel track along Vale Royal Drive, which becomes a tarmacked road at the end past Vale Royal Abbey and its golf course, and then reverts to gravel for a really scenic tour through the woods and alongside the river to reach the A556. Instead of trying to join the busy main road, follow the footpath/cycle lane up the hill until you reach Hartford Road, whereby you bear right and proceed into Davenham.

You now follow Route 573 for 5.5km along rural lanes and over the train line and the Trent and Mersey Canal to reach Lach Dennis for a right turn onto Birches Lane. At Lostock Green, you will need to cross over the A556 dual-carriageway, which will involve a dismount to cross via the pedestrian island to the right of the junction.

Birches Lane then continues northwards to Lostock Gralam, where you cross over the A559 onto Hall Lane to continue north to then turn right onto Dark Lane for the looping return on Budworth Heath Lane and Heath Lane to pass the Ice Cream Farm and arrive back into Great Budworth.

7) THE MID-CHESHIRE RIDGE - FROM WINSFORD

	Dist. (km)	Elev. (m)	m/km	Miles	Feet
Full Route	60.1	750	**12.5**	37.3	2461
Short Route	49.2	584	**11.9**	30.6	1916

Route Start-point: Winsford Cross Shopping Centre / Asda, Winsford

Stop-off Options: Tea Cosy Café (Frodsham); The Greedy Pig (Kelsall).

This route is in a quiet part of Cheshire and most of the route is set along very scenic and tranquil country lanes. The main geological feature of this route is the Mid-Cheshire Ridge, which is responsible for the route's four notable climbs, two of which feature in Simon Warren's Cycling Climbs of Northwest England.

This route also offers a shortcut option to further your route choice.

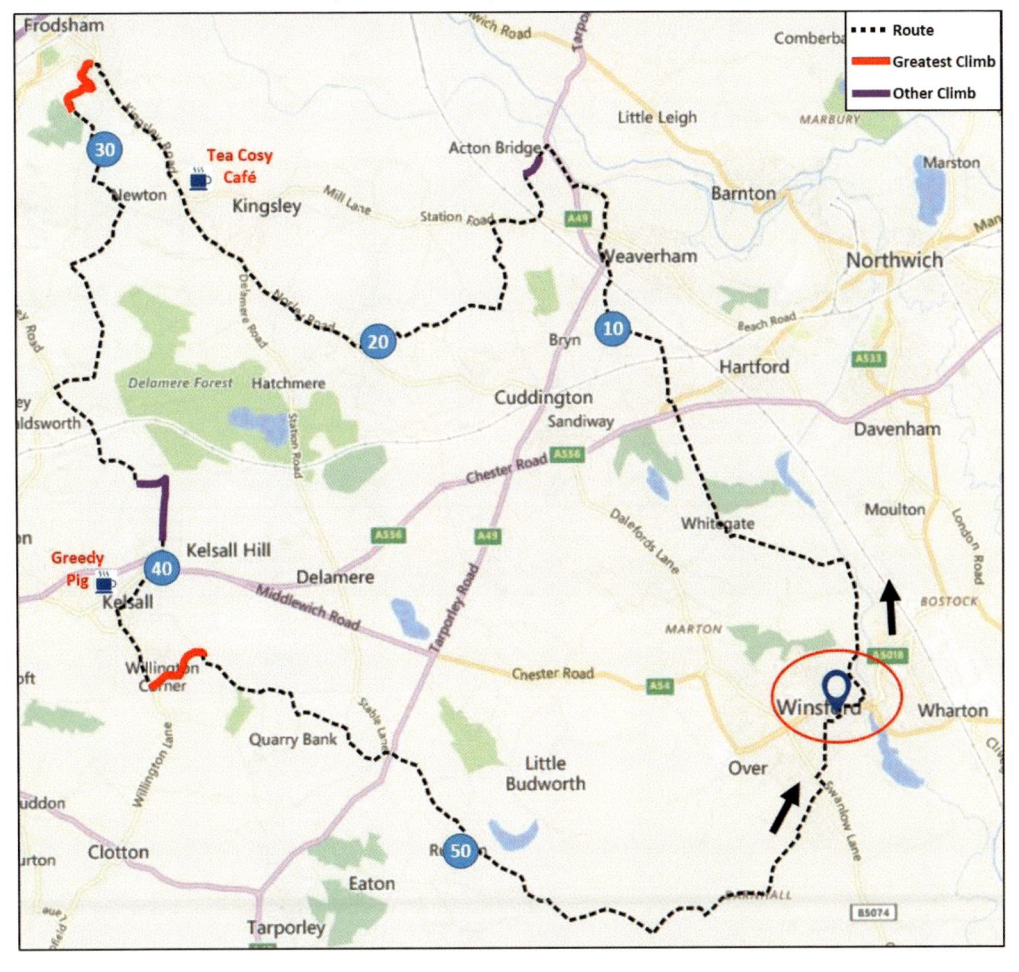

The Mid-Cheshire Ridge – from Winsford

The Low-down on the Climbs

The elevation profile for the route is illustrated in the diagram below, highlighting the climbs.

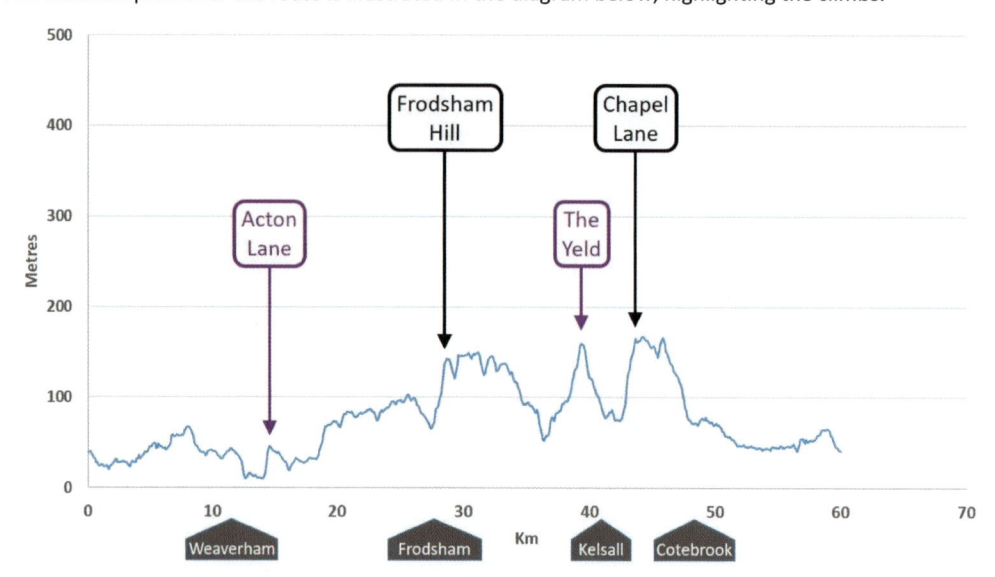

The vital statistics for the climbs are summarised in the table below.

Climb	Dist. (m)	Elev. (m)	Peak Gradient	CBB Index	Notes
Acton Lane	500	35	13%	17.0	Short but fairly steep
Frodsham Hill	1240	76	18%	18.2	Steep around the bends
The Yeld	900	62	14%	18.9	A very straight lane, steeper towards the top
Chapel Lane	1040	79	18%	22.2	Fairly steep, continuing further uphill after the official climb

The Mid-Cheshire Ridge – from Winsford

Shorter Route Option

There is one suggested option to shorten this route to 49.2km with 584m of climbing, which skips the loop around to Frodsham and the climb up Frodsham Hill.

The shortcut route follows the Cheshire Cycleway (Route 70) from Norley through Delamere Forest and re-joins the Full Route on Brines Brow Lane.

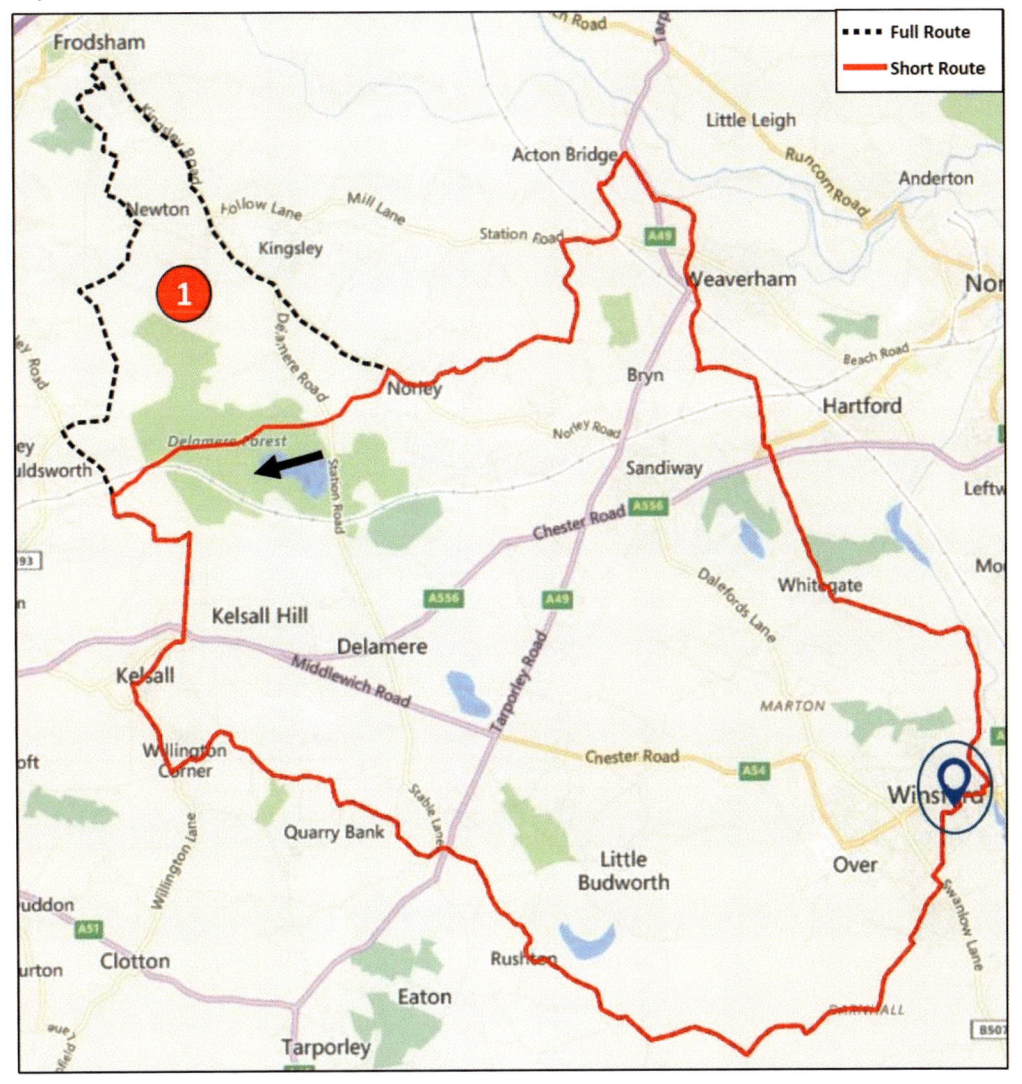

The corresponding reductions in distance and climbing are detailed in the table below.

	Dist. (km)	Miles	Elev. (m)	Feet
Shortcut	10.9	6.8	166	545

The Mid-Cheshire Ridge – from Winsford

Route Narrative

The route heads north from Winsford town centre, crossing the A54 and heading along the High Street to reach Bradford Road alongside the River Weaver. As you pass the Winsford Salt Mine, try to imagine that underground, the mine tunnels stretch for around 200km, reach a depth of 190m beneath ground level and have a total volume of 200 million cubic metres.

You then continue north through Whitegate, across a bridge over the A556 and onwards to reach Weaverham. There is a 500m section along the A49, followed by a left turn onto the Cheshire Cycleway on Acton Lane, just prior to the swing bridge over the Weaver. Soon after joining the lane, it starts to climb - reaching a peak gradient of 13%, but the climb is fairly short at 0.5km.

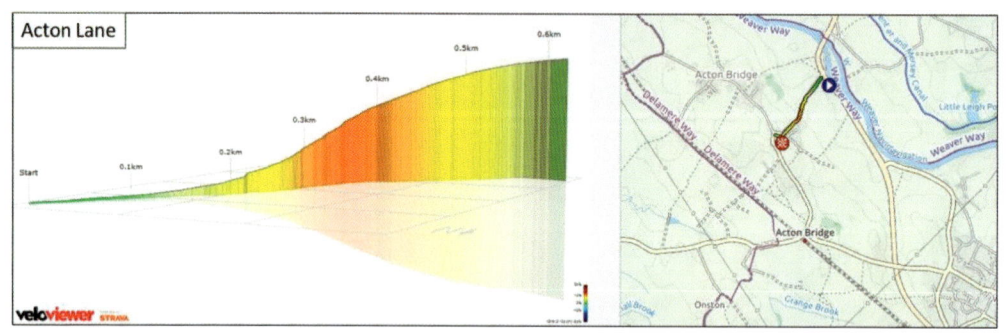

The route continues along the Cheshire Cycleway, with another short climb on the approach to Norley, after which the route joins the B5152 through to Frodsham - the location of the second notable climb up to the top of Frodsham Hill. This is much tamer (CBB = 18.2) than the big hills of the Peak District but it does peak at 18% gradient and has a series of twisting bends to negotiate.

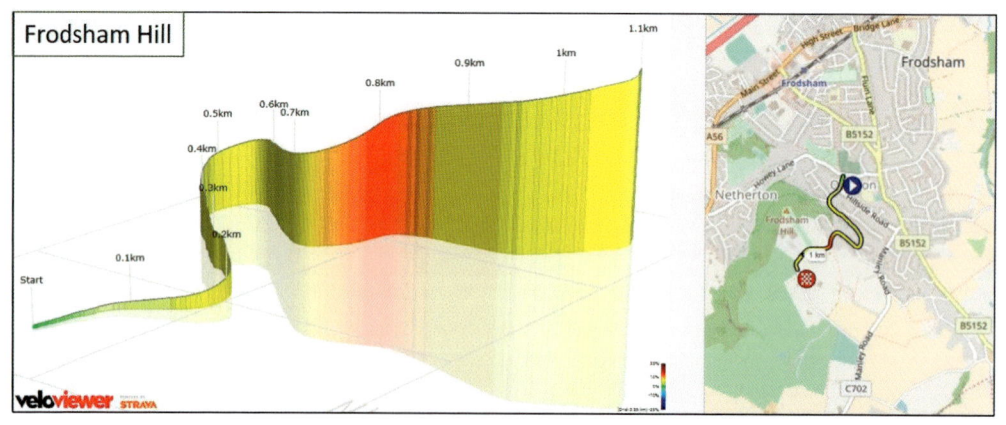

The route now heads south on a series of country lanes on top of the Mid Cheshire Ridge; a sandstone ridge dating back 225 million years providing great views over the Mersey Estuary and the Welsh hills.

The Mid-Cheshire Ridge – from Winsford

The route also joins a road section of Delamere Forest's "Fruits of the Forest" cycle route, which scales another popular climb called "The Yeld", which doesn't feature in The Cycling Climbs of North-West England but is definitely worthy of inclusion in this route (photo below).

The climbing starts as you turn onto Yeld Lane and travel in a dead-straight line heading almost due south. The climb peaks at around 14% gradient and reaches its summit by Mount Pleasant Gardens.

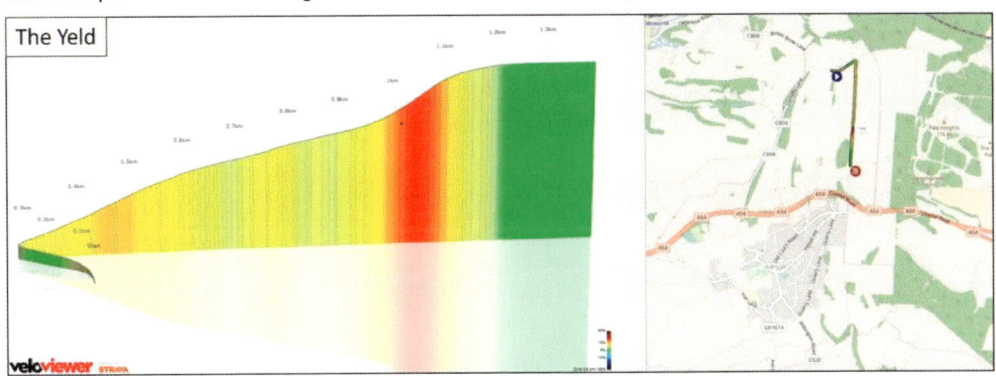

The Mid-Cheshire Ridge – from Winsford

The route then descends and turns right into Kelsall - a good place for a café stop if you need one - and then leads on to the base of the climb up Chapel Lane (photo below).

This is a slightly tougher climb than Frodsham Hill but still safely in the "Red" category.

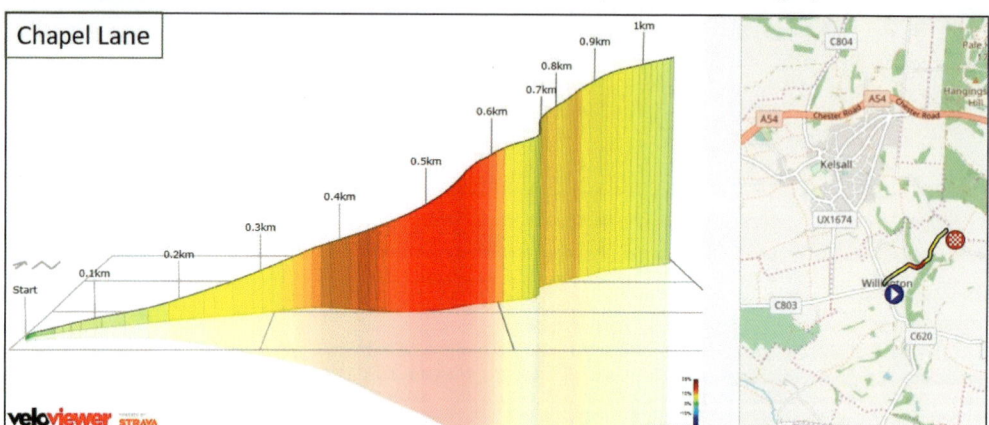

At the top, you're back onto the Fruits of the Forest route, going the other way around, and then descend from the ridge down to Cotebrook.

The route continues southeast through Rushton and around the side of the Oulton Park motor racing circuit and then by Ashcroft Airfield before joining Winsford Road for the return to the start.

8) UP MOW COP! - FROM MARTON

Dist. (km)	Elev. (m)	m/km	Miles	Feet
48	880	18.3	29.8	2887

Route Start-point: Chapeau! Café in Marton

Alternative Start-points: Congleton Garden Centre, Bosley

Stop-off Options: Congleton Garden Centre

This is a route with a mission: to climb Mow Cop – probably the toughest road-climb in Cheshire. There are four other notable climbs on the route, including Croker Hill (another of Simon Warren's greatest climbs) and Minn End Lane, which is Black-rated and very rural. As you would expect, the intensity metric is firmly in the Red at 18.3m/km.

Despite the above, the first 13.5km of the ride are relatively flat – giving you chance for a good warm-up – and so are the final 5km, for a cool-down!

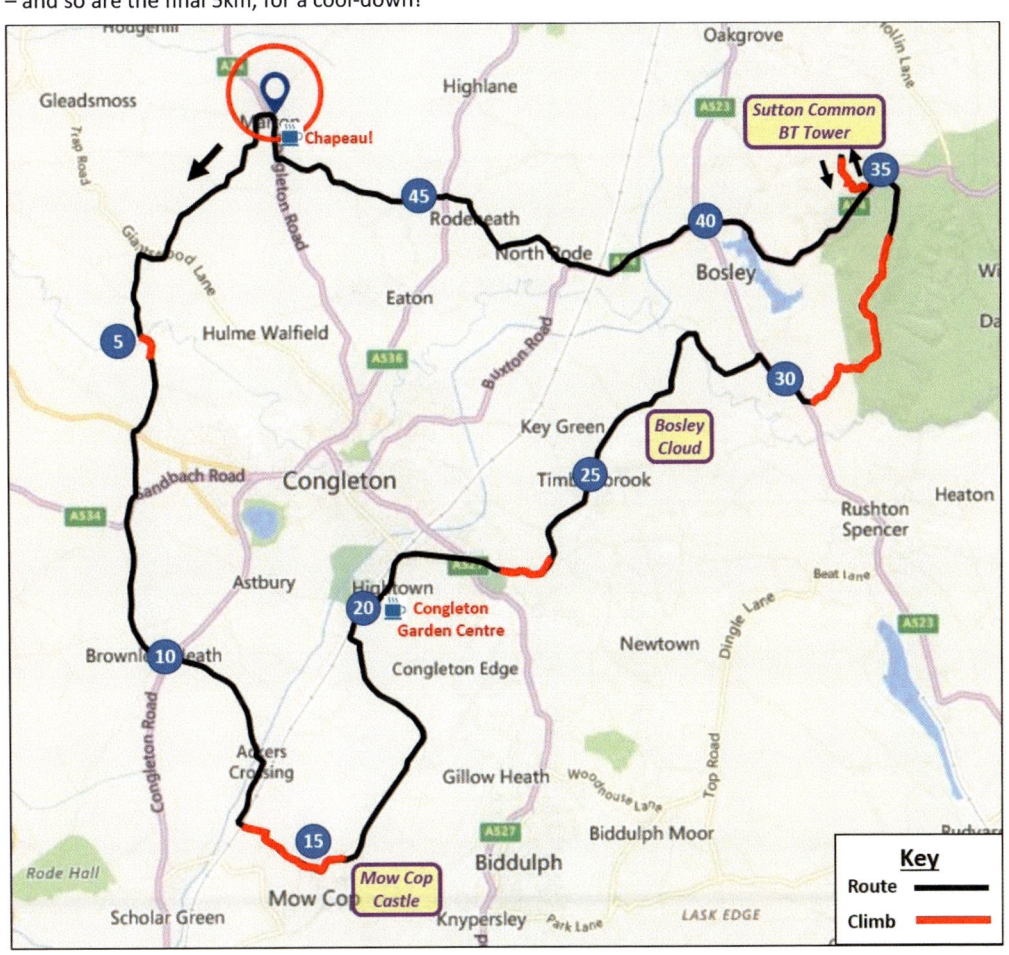

Up Mow Cop – from Marton

The Low-down on the Climbs

The elevation profile for the route is illustrated in the diagram below, highlighting the climbs.

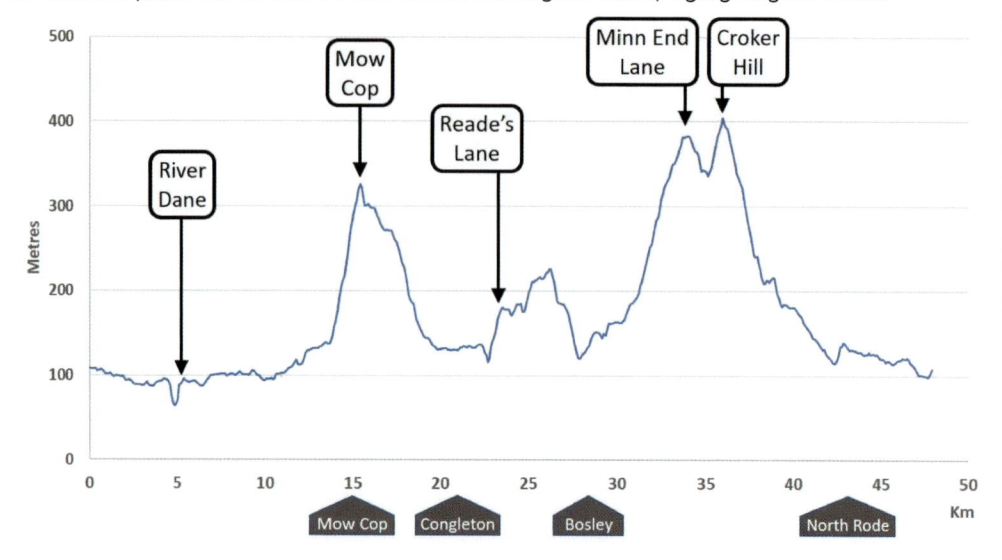

The vital statistics for the climbs are summarised in the table below.

Climb	Dist. (m)	Elev. (m)	Peak Gradient	CBB Index	Notes
River Dane	400	23	11%	13.2	Short but reasonably steep
Mow Cop	1830	199	27%	45.2	Probably the toughest road climb in Cheshire with a very steep section near the top
Reades Lane	1000	66	12%	18.6	Tougher than you are expecting!
Minn End Lane	2900	215	16%	33.7	Steep, loose and very rural with several gates along the way
Croker Hill	800	66	20%	22.7	Steep and bumpy with gates (and cows!)

Places of Interest on the Route

Mow Cop Castle
Originally built in 1754 as a summerhouse folly for the Wilbraham family, the castle has been the source of many disputes over land ownership and quarrying rights. In 1937, the castle was acquired by the National Trust. Remediation work took place in 2002-3 to secure the foundations and make-safe continued public access to the site.

Bosley Cloud
This is a distinctive landmark hill to the north of Congleton whose summit is at 343m above sea-level.

On the summer solstice from Leek, you can observe a double sunset – it first sets behind the summit of the hill, then reappears and finally sets on the horizon beyond.

Sutton Common BT Tower
This tower was built in the 1960s as part of the cold-war national line-of-sight Backbone communications infrastructure. The tower has a height of 72m and is made from reinforced concrete.

It is owned by BT and is now used for radio broadcasting.

Up Mow Cop – from Marton

Route Narrative

The route starts from the cycling-inspired Chapeau! cafe in Marton and follows the Cheshire Cycleway through a series of lanes in a southerly direction. After 5km, the route descends to cross the River Dane and then takes on the easiest of its notable climbs as you climb up the other side of the river valley.

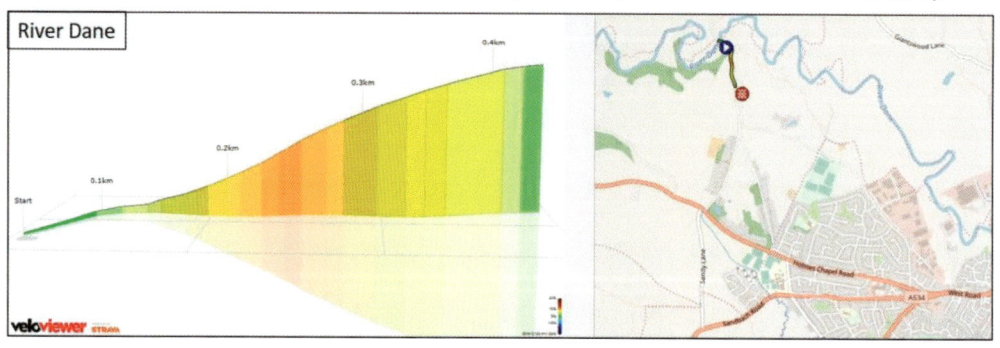

You then continue along Chelford Road, leaving the Cheshire Cycleway, and cross the A54 to join Sandy Lane, which leads onto the A534 for 0.4km. Walhill Lane then leads to a crossroads and onto Brownlow Heath Lane, which ends with a junction with the A34.

The next lane is New Road, which now offers a glimpse of the impending challenge as you spy the outline of the castle on the horizon (photo below).

The lane kicks up briefly as you cross over the Macclesfield Canal, it then rounds a bend and draws parallel with the railway line as the castle becomes closer. A left turn then takes you onto Drumber Lane to reach a level crossing – this is the start-point of the official Killer Mile climb, which plays host for both cycling and running hill-climb events.

Up Mow Cop – from Marton

The climb up Mow Cop has four notable sections: the initial section ramps up quite steep and twists around a pair of bends; the gradient for the second section then eases slightly – allowing you to find some rhythm, but keep some gas in the tank for what is to follow.

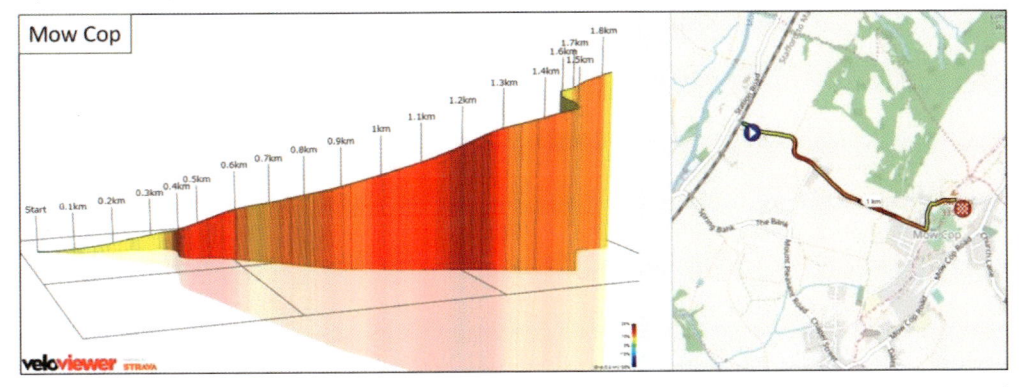

The third section is the star attraction, where the gradient ramps up to around 27% for a distance of 150m, as per the photo below.

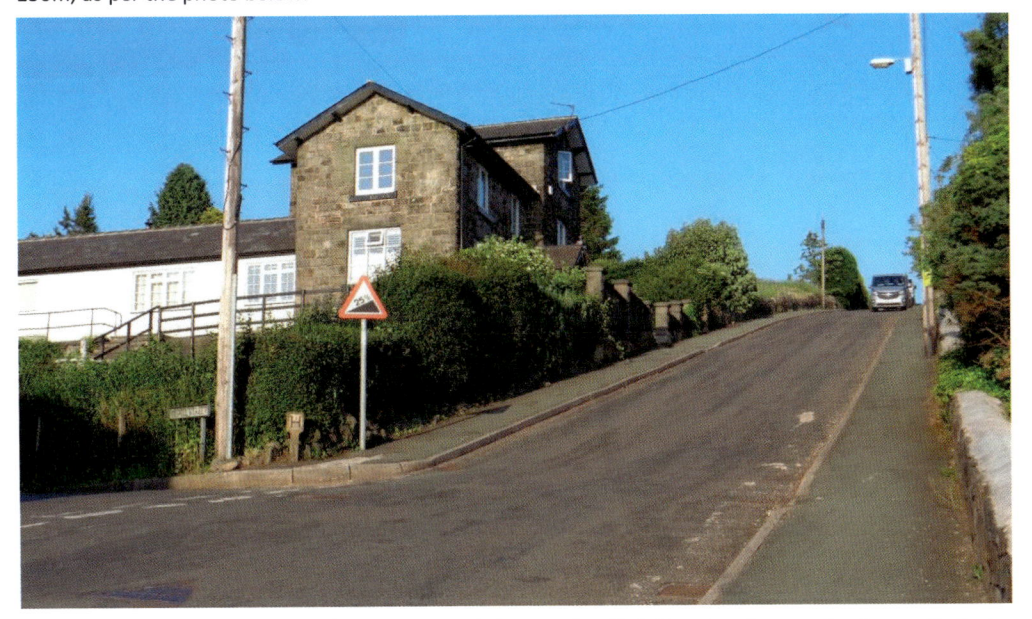

The gradient then levels out as the route turns left onto the High Street and passes by the castle, but a right turn at the end onto Wood Street brings on more climbing – to finish you off, as you scale the top of the hill to reach an elevation of 324m above sea-level. The descent down from the top is very steep and winding, with pot-holes and parked cars, so ride carefully to the junction with Congleton Road.

The route then follows the ridge, which marks the county border with Staffordshire, and swiftly descends Mow Lane to lead into the outskirts of Congleton. A right turn onto Leek Road leads to a junction with the A527 and across onto Reade's Lane for the next climb of the route.

Up Mow Cop – from Marton

This climb starts after crossing Dale-in-Shaw Brook and the Biddulph Valley Way (Route 55), it holds a fairly steady gradient of around 12% and continues for just short of a kilometre, so find the right gear and settle into your climbing rhythm.

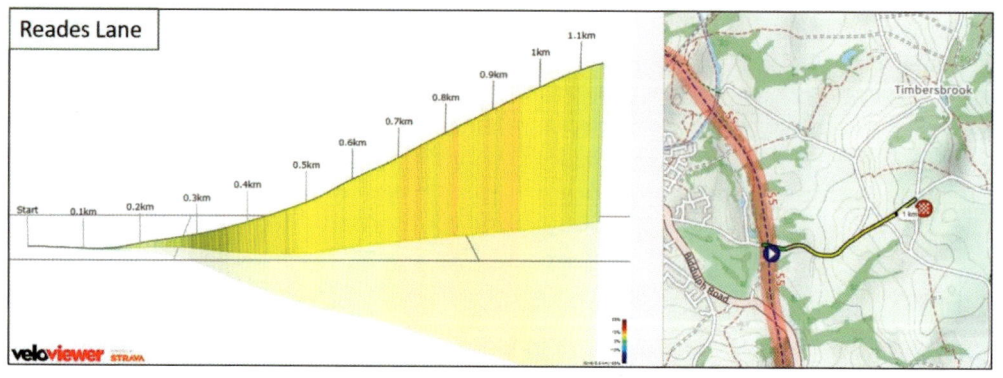

Near the top, the route bears left onto Under Rainow Road and then onto Tunstall Road, which continues to climb as you pass around the western side of Bosley Cloud. On reaching the northern tip of the hill, the road starts to descend to provide an exhilarating section down through the village of Bosley (scene of a disastrous fire in 2015) – but control your speed around the bends, especially if wet.

After a short climb to the end of Tunstall Road, the route turns right onto the A523 for 1km, leading you to a left turn onto Minn End Lane for another tough climb.

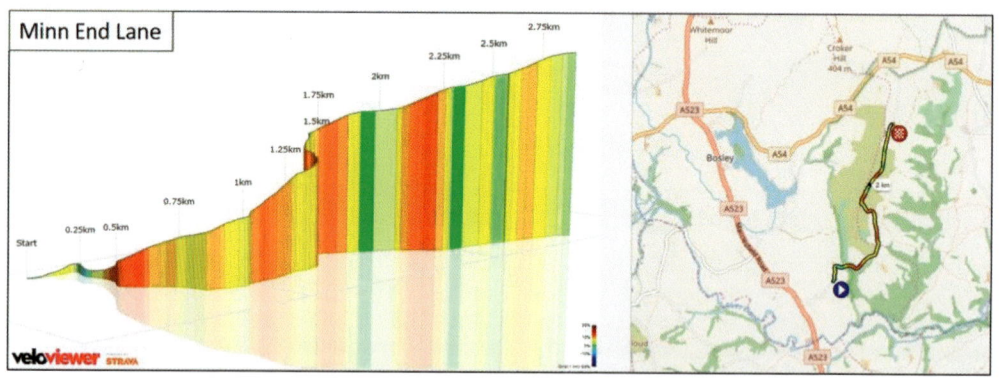

This is a long and winding climb on a tiny lane through fields of sheep and with great views of the local area. The road surface is fairly loose, so pick your line carefully on the steeper sections and around the bends. Note also that there are several gates along the lane that will require a dismount - please ensure the gates close properly behind you.

Up Mow Cop – from Marton

Once you reach the very top, you are treated to a 360° panoramic view for miles around (photo below).

There is a short descent down from the top of the hill, which is steep with a loose surface, so ride cautiously. At the end of the lane, the route turns left onto the A54 for 0.5km to reach the final climb of the ride.

The climb up Croker Hill is along a no-through lane, thus requiring you to retrace your way back down again. The surface of the lane is also strewn with potholes and there are several gates to negotiate. You therefore have an option whether to proceed with the climb or just continue with the route along the A54. The climb itself is fairly steep, levelling out towards the top – it does also offer great views on a clear day.

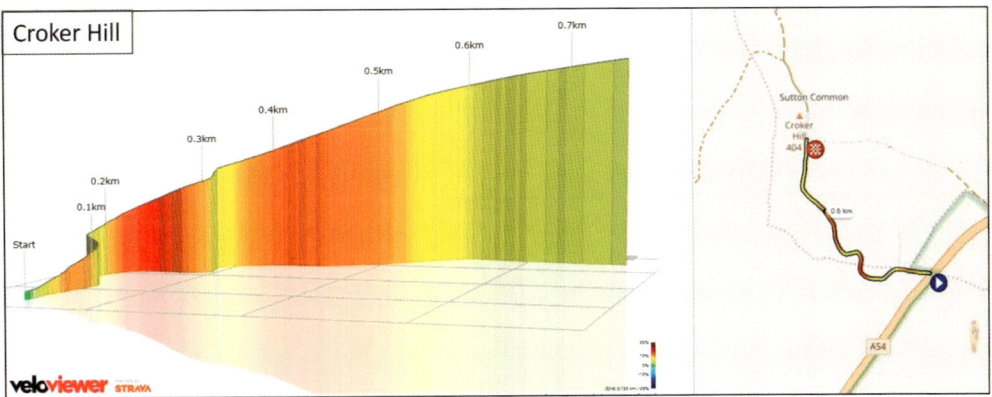

After returning from the climb, you then turn right onto the A54 for a white-knuckle descent to reach the junction with the A523. You then proceed across the junction and continue downhill for a further 2km to reach a right-turn onto Church Lane for a short, sharp climb.

The route then continues to follow a series of country lanes, crossing over the A536 onto Cocksmoss Lane to reach the A34 for the final 0.6km return to Marton.

9) BIG HILLS CIRCUIT – FROM ALDERLEY EDGE

Dist. (km)	Elev. (m)	m/km	Miles	Feet
53.8	983	**18.3**	33.4	3225

Route Start-point: Alderley Edge

Alternative Start-points: Prestbury, Bollington, Sutton, Gawsworth

Stop-off Options: Wizard Tea Rooms (Over Alderley), Chocolate Box Café (Prestbury), Crag Inn (Wildboarclough), Gawsworth Shop, Flora (Henbury).

This route is a combination of the Full and Short Routes of Stage 1 of the Cheshire Cycleway (as detailed further in "Riding the Cheshire Cycleway") to make a really challenging circuit that starts and finishes in Alderley Edge. The route includes the three Black-rated climbs of Blaze Hill, Ankers Knoll Lane and Nabbs Road; it also goes both up and down the Red-rated Artists Lane. It can be ridden in either direction; clockwise is steeper for the ascents and conversely anti-clockwise has more demanding descents.

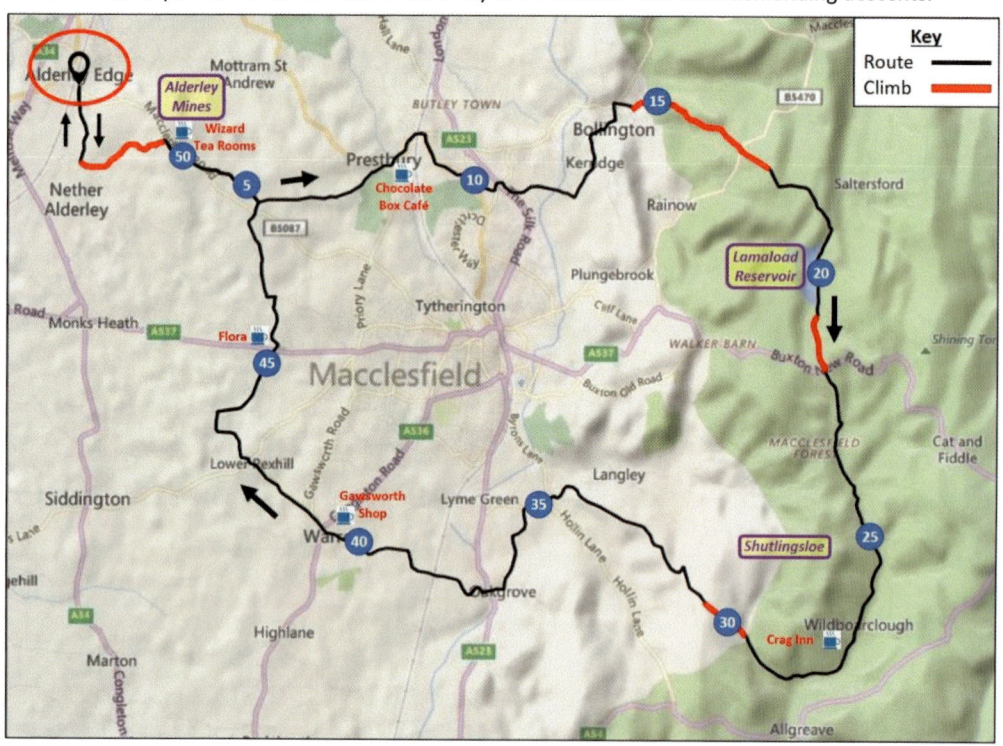

The route has a Red intensity of 18.3m/km and contains four notable climbs, as summarised below.

Climb	Dist. (m)	Elev. (m)	Peak Gradient	CBB Index	Notes
Artists Lane	1770	86	10%	15.7	Gentle start, one steeper section
Blaze Hill & Pike Road	3200	239	20%	36.0	Very steep then flat then steep again
Ankers Knoll Lane	900	96	25%	32.5	Brutally steep at the start
Nabbs Road	700	90	21%	38.0	Shorter but consistently very steep

Big Hills Circuit – From Alderley Edge

The Low-down on the Climbs
The elevation profile for the route is illustrated in the diagram below, highlighting the climbs.

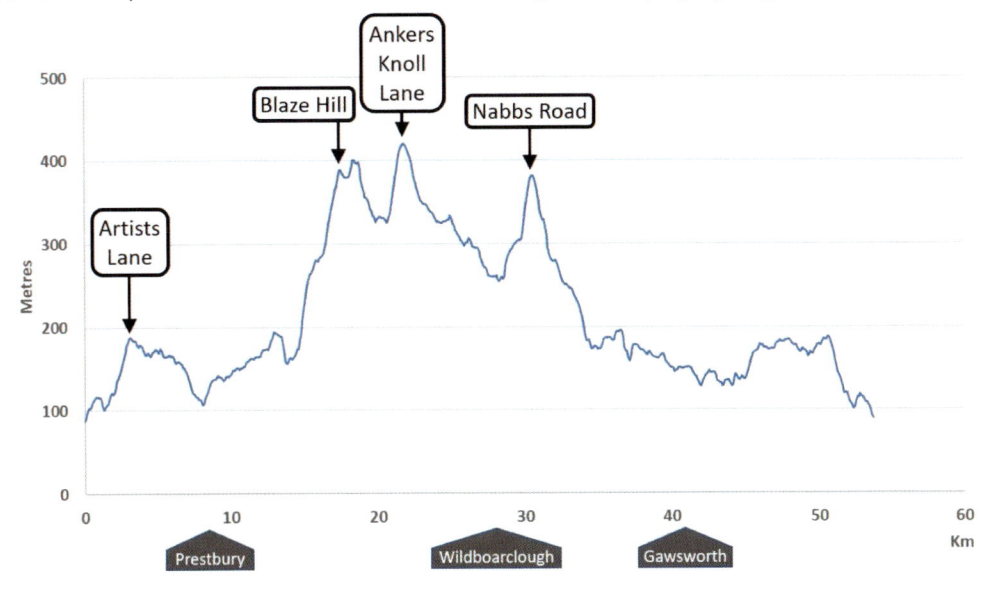

Places of Interest on the Route

Alderley Edge Mines
The hill above the village of Alderley Edge is formed mainly from Sandstone, however within the sandstone and the faults through the rock there are deposits of minerals that have been mined for around 4000 years. The most common metals extracted from the mineral rocks are copper, lead and cobalt, but there have even been small amounts of gold discovered here!

Underground, there is a vast network of shafts and passages with one of the mines (West Mine) having around 10km of tunnels.

Archaeological discoveries have revealed Bronze Age smelting equipment (c. 2000BC), evidence of Roman activity as well as more extensive finds from the 18th and 19th centuries. The site is now owned by the National Trust, if you wish to visit the mines then this needs to be arranged through Derbyshire Caving Club.

https://www.derbyscc.org.uk/alderley/index.php

Lamaload Reservoir
This reservoir, at 305m (1000'), has the highest constructed dam in England. It contains around 2 billion litres of water when full and is a site popular with walkers, birdwatchers and fishermen.

Shutlingsloe
A very distinctive landmark, known as the "Cheshire Matterhorn", with a very different profile depending on your viewpoint. Its summit is 506m (1660') above sea-level, making it the third highest peak in Cheshire.

Big Hills Circuit – From Alderley Edge

Route Narrative

This ride starts from the village of Alderley Edge, one corner of Cheshire's Golden Triangle - amid the bars, cafes and Ferraris! As you leave the village along Congleton Road (the old A34 before the creation of the bypass) the tone of the stage is set as the road rises, forcing a change of gears as you climb around 30m (100') and pass the big set-back houses with commanding views over the Cheshire Plain.

After a short descent, the route turns left onto Artists Lane - the first challenge of the ride, which starts gently but gets steeper towards the top.

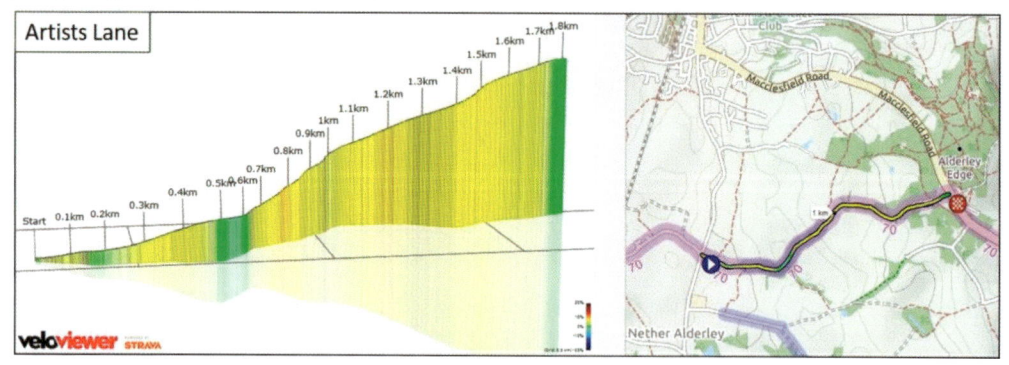

At the top, you arrive at the Wizard pub and turn right for a short stretch along the main road - note the National Trust car park leading to the Edge itself and the old mines. The route then bears left past Hare Hill and onwards towards Prestbury - another corner of Cheshire's Golden Triangle (the 3rd one being Wilmslow). The descent into Prestbury is down Chelford Road, which is fairly steep with a number of grids and drain covers to dodge on the way down.

The route goes through Prestbury village - with cobbled speed-bumps, kicks upwards briefly as you pass the train station and continues to a junction with the A523. After negotiating the roundabout and right-turn, you join Clarke Lane and head out into the countryside once more, passing the Lord Clyde pub and crossing over both the Middlewood Way and the Macclesfield Canal (photo below).

Big Hills Circuit – From Alderley Edge

Clarke Lane joins with Oak Lane which rises further up to the Bull's Head in Kerridge as the road becomes Jackson Lane, turning right at the end for a very steep descent down Lord Street into Bollington. At the roundabout the route turns onto Ingersley Road which rises steeply after the Poachers Inn - stretching the lungs ready for the first major climb of Blaze Hill.

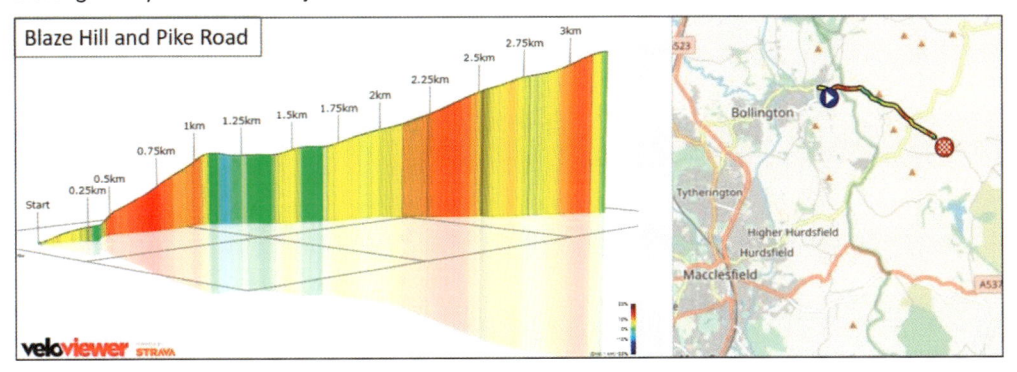

At the top of Blaze Hill (photo below), the route crosses the B5470 (take care at junction) and continues upwards along Pike Road, following the signs towards the Goyt Valley.

After descending Erwin Lane, (known as Deadman's Hill – particularly if riding anti-clockwise!) the route bears right at a triangle junction - sparing you from an even more brutal climb up to Pym's Chair if you were to bear left! You then follow a picturesque lane passing sheep grazing in fields and Lamaload Reservoir on the right-hand side.

Big Hills Circuit – From Alderley Edge

Just as you become at-one with the world, the road rises sharply upwards forcing an abrupt gear shift & battle for traction to climb the very steep start of Ankers Knoll Lane.

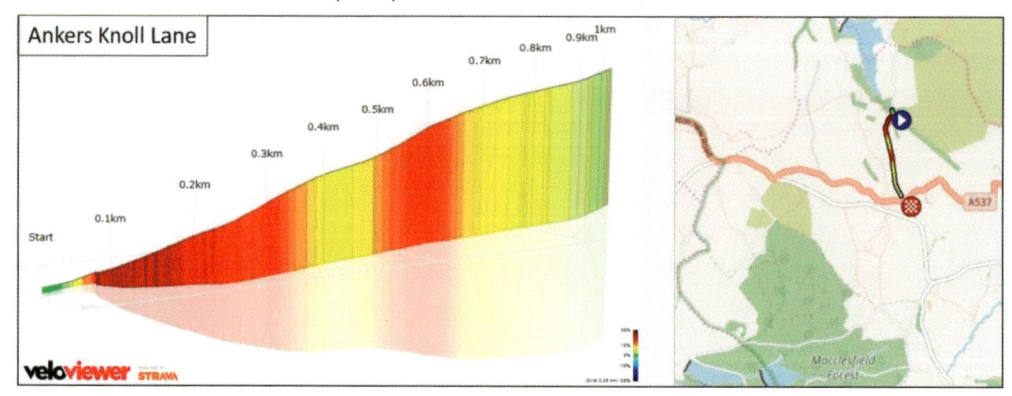

The top of Ankers Knoll Lane is the highest point of the whole Cheshire Cycleway at 417m (1375') above sea-level and rewards you with fantastic views across Cheshire and the Peak District, in particular the notable peak of Shutlingsloe at 506m (1660'). The route then crosses the A537 and descends Ankers Lane - beware of the tight left-hand bend and immediate right-turn at the bottom, just by the Stanley Arms pub.

The next seven kilometres treat you to a picture-postcard ride to Wildboarclough (photo below), with a slight downwards gradient alongside the streams of Tor Brook and Clough Brook, passing by The Crag Inn.

Big Hills Circuit – From Alderley Edge

After you leave the streams, the route turns right, the scenery changes to rolling farmland again and you need to prepare yourself for the final major climb of Nabbs Road, which starts steep and eases towards the top.

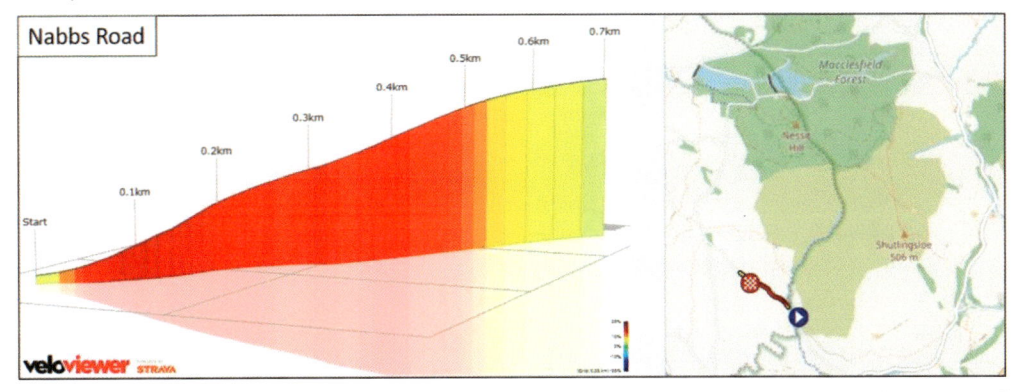

The well-earned descent passes the Hanging Gate pub, the highest pub in Cheshire and with a history of around 400 years; as you continue down Ridge Hill (photo below) and look to your right, you are treated to great views of Macclesfield Forest and Tegg's Nose. Take care as you approach the bottom of Ridge Hill as the route turns sharply onto Church Lane and into the village of Sutton.

The route then joins the Leek Old Road (the former main road before the A523 was constructed), passes Sutton Reservoir and kicks upwards for a short climb before crossing the A523 and the Macclesfield canal via a swing bridge (you can still cross the canal if the bridge is open via the footbridge, but this involves carrying your bike up and over the bridge). After a short climb up from the canal, the route leads to the village of Gawsworth (which has a shop that serves food and hot drinks if you wish to stop).

In order to complete the loop back to Alderley Edge, the route now follows the "via Henbury" option of the Cheshire Cycleway, which crosses the A536 onto Dark Lane and then dog-legs across Pexhill Road onto Bearhurst Lane and School Lane to arrive in Henbury at the junction with the A537 (and opposite Flora Café).

You then climb (much more gently than earlier) up through a series of lanes to Over Alderley and retrace your outbound route down Artists Lane (take care on the bends) and up-and-over Congleton Road to return into Alderley Edge.

10) MACC FOREST – FROM MACCLESFIELD

Dist. (km)	Elev. (m)	m/km	Miles	Feet
33.1	823	24.9	20.6	2700

Route Start-point: Macclesfield Town Centre

Alternative Start-points: Macc Forest Visitor Centre, Rainow, Kerridge, Bollington

For a relatively short ride, this certainly packs a few punches (with its Black Intensity metric) - not ideal as a taster for newcomers to off-road riding, but fantastic if you want a challenge amid stunning scenery!

The two big climbs are along fire-tracks through Macclesfield Forest, which are reasonably firm and drain well after rain. Judy Lane and Heathcote Lane are road climbs, Kiskhill Lane and White Nancy are on tracks but with firm surfaces. Most of the steep descending is on roads - unless you choose to ride the route in the other direction.

The Low-down on the Climbs

The elevation profile for the route is illustrated in the diagram below, highlighting the key climbs and off-road sections.

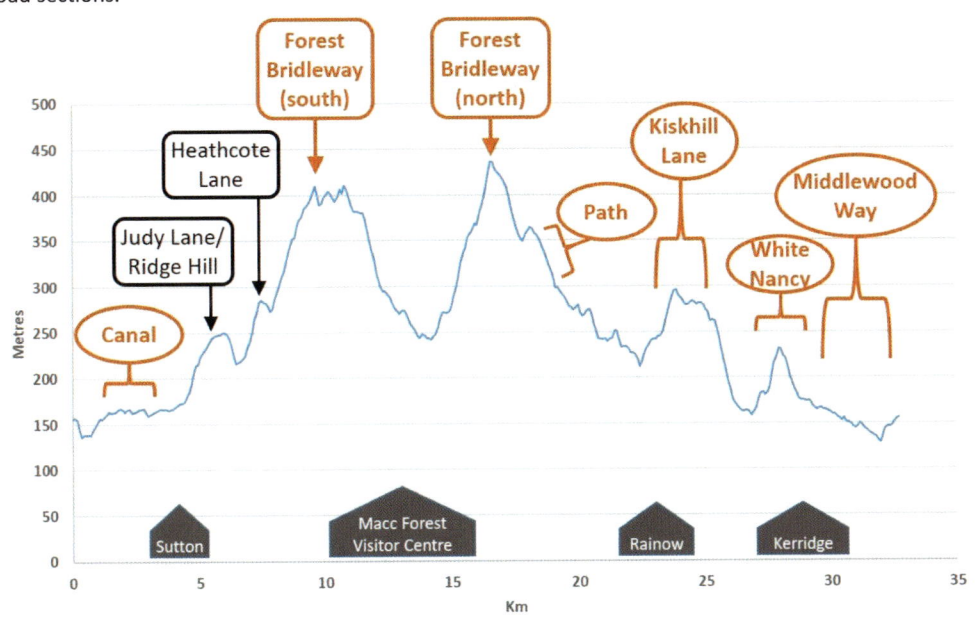

There are six notable climbs, including three Blacks, on this route, their vital statistics are listed below.

Climb	Distance (m)	Elevation Gain (m)	Peak Gradient	CBB Index	Features
Judy Lane + Ridge Hill (short)	1250	72	13%	16.9	Steep at the start
Heathcote Lane	460	59	23%	33.7	Short but very steep towards the top
Forest Bridleway (south)	1650	127	29%	26.8	Very steep section near the start of the bridle path
Forest Bridleway (north)	2300	205	25%	38.4	Very steep towards the top
Kiskhill Lane	470	58	20%	32.3	Steep but steady climb
White Nancy	370	43	24%	28.6	Steep but fairly short

Macc Forest – From Macclesfield

Route Narrative

The route departs south and east from the town centre along a mix of minor roads and footpaths to join the Macclesfield Canal from Black Road, and then heads south along the towpath to Sutton. You then cut through a farm towards the first climb of the ride, which ascends Judy Lane and continues up Ridge Hill until the left turn onto Wetton Way.

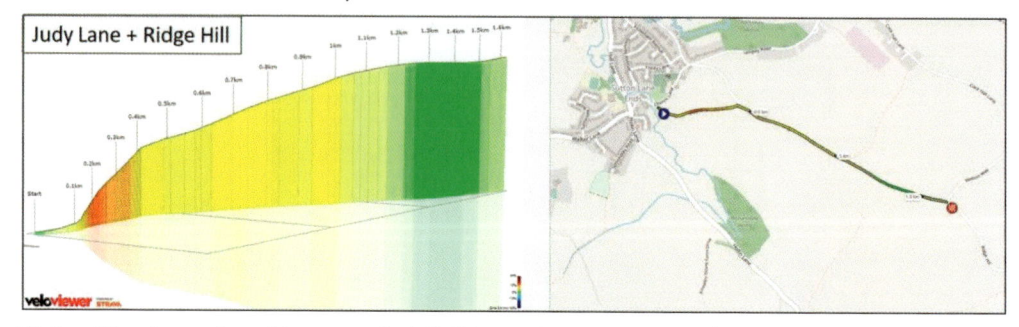

Wetton Way descends and becomes Cock Hall Lane, the route turns right just before the corner onto Heathcote Lane for the second climb of the ride - a short but very steep climb with a "Black" CBB rating.

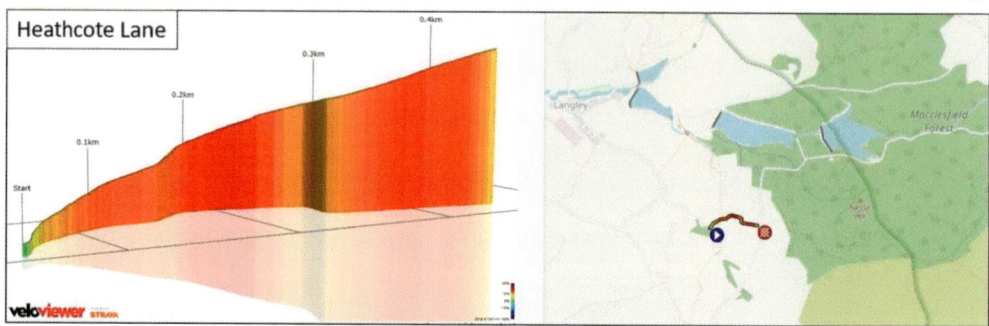

At the (very steep) top, turn left and follow the lane into the forest, turning immediately right after the sharp right corner onto the Forest Bridleway.

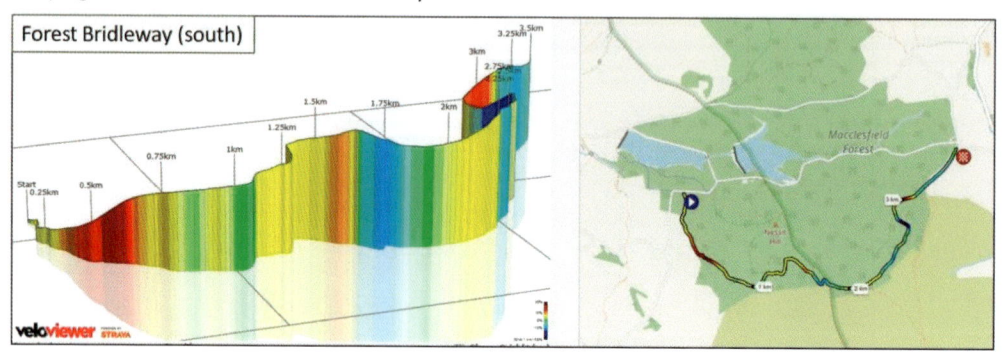

Macc Forest – From Macclesfield

This is a 3.5km trail that starts steep and meanders through the trees and then rises clear of the trees to over 400m above sea-level to provide fantastic viewpoints - as per the photographs below.

At the end of the bridle path, you turn left for a steep descent down Standing Stone Road, pass by the forest visitor centre and reservoirs as far as the Leather's Smithy pub and then take a sharp right turn onto Charity Lane.

The route follows the road for 500m and then takes a left through a gate onto the way-marked "Forest Bridleway" for the next ordeal.

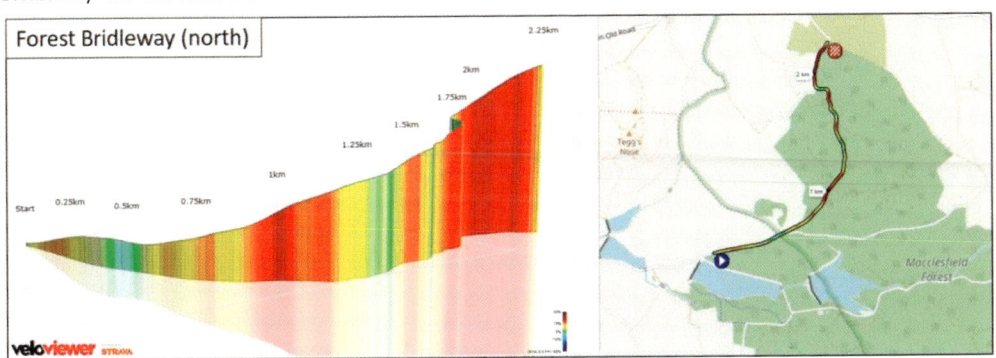

Macc Forest – From Macclesfield

This section starts reasonably gently, steepens towards the middle and then really ramps up to around 25% gradient towards the end of the trail. If that wasn't enough, there is then a further 350m-long section of really steep (20%) ascent to the top of Hacked Way Lane to conquer to finish the climb.

The next off-road section follows a right turn just before Teggs Nose Visitor Centre. This time is straight down the hill, which is not too steep but it is bumpy in places. More descending follows along a series of lanes to reach Kiskhill Lane for another dose of climbing. The road surface is fairly poor for a lane but not quite into the category of a bridle path, the lane is also steep - reaching 20% gradient in places.

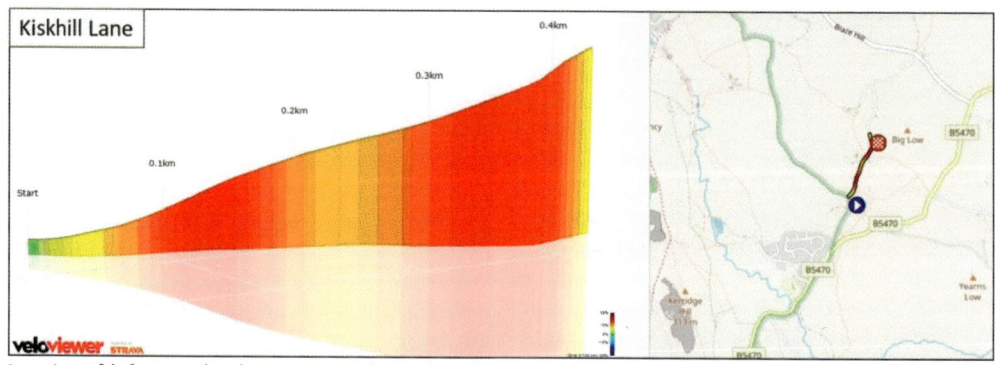

A series of left turns leads onto Ingersley Vale, which turns from road to gravel track as you follow the River Dean upstream. When you reach a junction, you need to follow the track around to the right and up the hill. This is the final climb of the ride and it delivers quite a punch as the lane progressively steepens up to around 20% gradient.

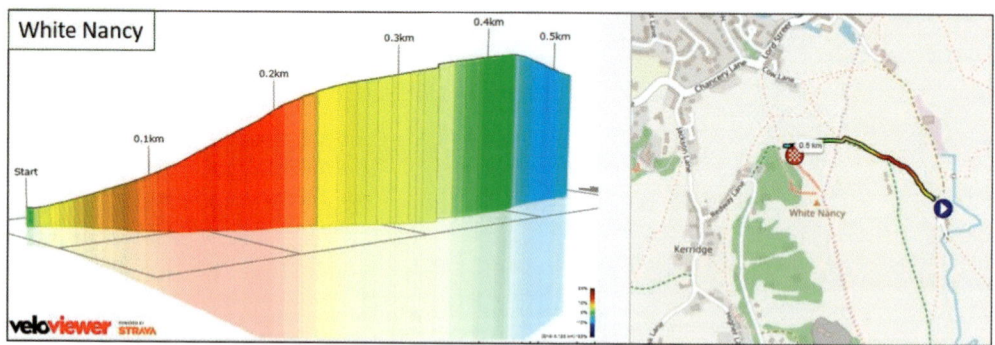

The descent is equally steep but not very long and exits onto Redway Lane, which joins Jackson Lane by the Bulls Head pub - a good place for a pint if you're in need of one! The route turns left and descends away from Kerridge along Oak Lane. Immediately after the sharp right-hand bend, there is a turning onto a path on the left which then leads down and over the Macclesfield Canal and joins up with the Middlewood Way (Route 55). There is a bit of an obstacle course to negotiate as you cross the bridge over the Silk Road, after which it's a fairly smooth run along the tarmacked path parallel to the main road. Just after crossing the River Bollin, you reach a T-junction - turn right and follow the path onto Summerlea Close, which then leads onto Manchester Road for your return to the start.

ROUTE SUMMARY AND DOWNLOAD LINKS

The table below provides a summary of the routes in terms of distance, elevation gain and intensity as well as links to the .gpx files.

Route	Dist. (km)	Elev. (m)	m/km	Download Links
Carden Park	53.3	433	8.1	https://ukcycleroutes.com/cc-eg-carden/
Audlem	82	551	6.7	https://ukcycleroutes.com/audlem/
Tatton 80k	80.5	629	7.8	https://ukcycleroutes.com/tatton_80k/
Portal 100k	100	804	8.0	https://ukcycleroutes.com/portal_100km/
Laureen's Combo	60.9	416	6.8	https://ukcycleroutes.com/double_laureen/
Budworth Loop	63.1	690	10.9	https://ukcycleroutes.com/budworth/
Mid-Cheshire Ridge	60.1	750	12.5	https://ukcycleroutes.com/winsford/
Mow Cop	48	876	18.3	https://ukcycleroutes.com/mow_cop/
CC Big Hills	53.8	983	18.3	https://ukcycleroutes.com/cc-eg-big_hills/
Macc Forest Gravel	33.1	823	24.9	https://ukcycleroutes.com/macc_gravel_33k/

How to Use the Download link

Each route has a download link, this will enable you to download a .gpx file to your local device (e.g. PC or phone).

You will then need to determine the required format of file for your navigation device. Some devices (e.g. Garmin Edge 800 series) will accept a .gpx file directly. Others will require an interim file conversion stage, for example:

- Garmin Edge 500 series work best with a .tcx file
- Garmin Edge 25 devices require a .fit file

There are numerous websites available that will perform the conversion for you, such as: https://www.gpsies.com/convert.do

The .gpx files also include turn-by-turn directions (as well as the usual "breadcrumb trail"), which have been tested on my Garmin device, but please check they load correctly on your navigation device if you intend to rely on the directions during your ride.

Other titles available by Dave Peart:

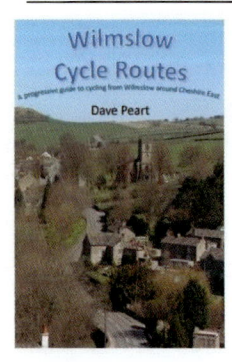

Wilmslow Cycle Routes
25 routes graded in order of difficulty that start from Wilmslow, ranging from 5-45 miles.

Available from:
- ukcycleroutes.com
- Amazon

Serious Cycling: Macclesfield
22 stunning routes that start from Macclesfield, ranging from 30-200km.

Available from:
- ukcycleroutes.com
- Amazon

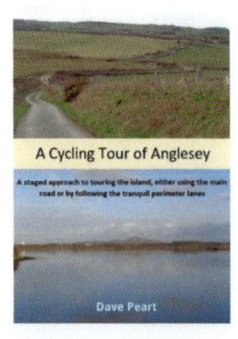

A Cycling Tour of Anglesey
A staged approach to touring the island, either on the main road or by following the perimeter lanes.

Available from:
- ukcycleroutes.com
- Amazon

Serious Climbing: Macclesfield
Seven challenging routes that encompass 48 of the UK's Greatest Cycling Climbs from Simon Warren's books.

Available from:
- ukcycleroutes.com
- Amazon

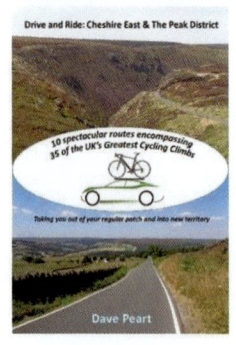

Drive and Ride: Cheshire East & The Peak District
10 routes just that bit further away from the Macclesfield area – but worth putting the bike in the car to ride.

Available from:
- ukcycleroutes.com
- Amazon

How to Set Up Your Home Gym
A modular approach to setting up a gym at home to suit your space, budget and exercise programme.

Available from:
- Amazon

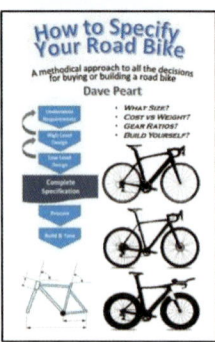

How to Specify Your Road Bike
A methodical approach for buying or building a road bike.

Available from:
- How2specabike.com
- Amazon

How to Specify Your Mountain Bike
A methodical approach for buying or building a mountain bike.

Available from:
- How2specabike.com
- Amazon

https://ukcycleroutes.com/

https://www.amazon.co.uk/Dave-Peart/e/B07H2PJCKM

Printed in Poland
by Amazon Fulfillment
Poland Sp. z o.o., Wrocław